W9-BZW-223

EDIBLE FLOWERS

Edible

Series Editor: Andrew F. Smith

EDIBLE is a revolutionary series of books dedicated to food and drink that explores the rich history of cuisine. Each book reveals the global history and culture of one type of food or beverage.

Already published

Apple Erika Janik *Banana* Lorna Piatti-Farnell
Barbecue Jonathan Deutsch and Megan J. Elias
Beef Lorna Piatti-Farnell *Beer* Gavin D. Smith
Brandy Becky Sue Epstein *Bread* William Rubel
Cake Nicola Humble *Caviar* Nichola Fletcher
Champagne Becky Sue Epstein *Cheese* Andrew Dalby
Chillies Heather Arndt Anderson *Chocolate* Sarah Moss
and Alexander Badenoch *Cocktails* Joseph M. Carlin
Curry Colleen Taylor Sen *Dates* Nawal Nasrallah
Doughnut Heather Delancey Hunwick *Dumplings* Barbara Gallani
Edible Flowers Constance L. Kirker and Mary Newman
Eggs Diane Toops *Fats* Michelle Phillipov *Figs* David C. Sutton
Game Paula Young Lee *Gin* Lesley Jacobs Solmonson
Hamburger Andrew F. Smith *Herbs* Gary Allen
Hot Dog Bruce Kraig *Ice Cream* Laura B. Weiss
Lamb Brian Yarvin *Lemon* Toby Sonneman
Lobster Elisabeth Townsend *Melon* Sylvia Lovegren
Milk Hannah Velten *Mushroom* Cynthia D. Bertelsen
Nuts Ken Albala *Offal* Nina Edwards *Olive* Fabrizia Lanza
Onions and Garlic Martha Jay *Oranges* Clarissa Hyman
Pancake Ken Albala *Pasta and Noodles* Kantha Shelke *Pie* Janet Clarkson
Pineapple Kaori O' Connor *Pizza* Carol Helstosky
Pork Katharine M. Rogers *Potato* Andrew F. Smith
Pudding Jeri Quinzio *Rice* Renee Marton *Rum* Richard Foss
Salad Judith Weinraub *Salmon* Nicolaas Mink *Sandwich* Bee Wilson
Sauces Maryann Tebben *Sausage* Gary Allen *Soup* Janet Clarkson
Spices Fred Czarra *Sugar* Andrew F. Smith *Tea* Helen Saberi
Tequila Ian Williams *Truffle* Zachary Nowak
Vodka Patricia Herlihy *Water* Ian Miller
Whiskey Kevin R. Kosar *Wine* Marc Millon

Edible Flowers

A Global History

Constance L. Kirker and Mary Newman

REAKTION BOOKS

Property of Gloucester County Library

Published by Reaktion Books Ltd
Unit 32, Waterside
44–48 Wharf Road
London N1 7UX, UK
www.reaktionbooks.co.uk

First published 2016

Copyright © Constance L. Kirker and Mary Newman 2016

All rights reserved
No part of this publication may be reproduced, stored in a retrieval
system, or transmitted, in any form or by any means, electronic,
mechanical, photocopying, recording or otherwise, without the prior
permission of the publishers

Printed and bound in China by 1010 Printing International Ltd

A catalogue record for this book is available from the British Library

ISBN 978 1 78023 638 4

Contents

Introduction 7

1 The Ancient World 14

2 The Middle Ages to the Nineteenth Century 26

3 The Victorian Era to Today 40

4 Asia 54

5 The Mediterranean and the Middle East 71

6 Europe 89

7 The Americas 111

Afterword 129

Precautions When Eating Edible Flowers 131

Flower Dinner Menu 135

Recipes 139

Select Bibliography 149

Websites and Associations 151

Acknowledgements 155

Photo Acknowledgements 157

Index 159

Introduction

Perhaps it was luck, or maybe it was the work of the Kitchen Gods. After all, it is during Tet – the Vietnamese New Year – when the Kitchen Gods report the doings of mortals to the ruler of the spirit realm. Whatever the explanation, it was serendipitous that, after five weeks researching edible flowers in Southeast Asia, we stumbled upon a brand new restaurant in Ho Chi Minh City named Chi Hoa. In Vietnamese *hoa* means 'flower' and the first thing we noticed on the menu was *lau hoa*, flower hotpot. This was where we were meant to be.

Stunning fresh blossoms of squash, daylilies, white *so dua* flowers, lotus stems and yellow velvetleaf buds made up the floral ingredients in our flower hotpot. All of these were cooked together in a light pineapple soup base that included chunks of salmon. The restaurant's brochure explained why the name had been chosen: '*Chi Hoa*, which means "flowers", is a common name of many Vietnamese women who are sophisticated, caring and always bring great love into every meal they cook for their family.' The friendly and accommodating manager of this shiny new restaurant summarized his philosophy for us: 'Yes . . . we treat you like you are part of our family.' His statement echoed precisely what we had learned in our research about the power of flowers in relationship to the food we eat. Everywhere in the world, both historically and in contemporary cuisines, the use of flowers in food has been special and exceptional and the flowers themselves have always been included with intent and care, never accidentally or without purpose. Flowers are used in food by someone who cares about you, and who cares about the beauty of what you are about to eat.

What is it that makes flowers, which often have only a hint of taste or flavour, such powerful ingredients in culinary traditions throughout human history? How have they been used since the time of the first prehistoric, primitive foragers to sophisticated court chefs of the medieval period? Why are edible flowers having such a resurgence in cuisines today, from proponents of the farm-to-table movement to contemporary kings of molecular gastronomy?

Researchers of behavioural science have shown that the presentation of flowers to someone almost always guarantees

During Tet in Vietnam, the Kitchen Gods report to the ruler of the spirit realm the doings of the household for that year. These kitchen gods were purchased in a market in Hue, Vietnam.

Flower hotpot, a speciality at Chi Hoa restaurant, Ho Chi Minh City, Vietnam.

a Duchenne smile – a facial expression of genuine pleasure. Any mother, hostess or chef can testify that beautifully presented food will elicit such a smile. Flowers on the table are a must, flowers as a garnish on a plate a lovely surprise, but the idea of flowers as an integral culinary ingredient is much less familiar to us. This book explores the history of edible

Aztec forager, sketch from the 16th-century Florentine Codex. Since earliest times, man has foraged for edible flowers.

flowers and encourages everyone to try flower power in their cooking.

For the purposes of this book, we are defining a flower simply as the seed-bearing part of a plant: this consists of stamens, which are coated with pollen, the male 'seed' of the flower; and pistils, the reproductive organs of the plant, which are surrounded by brightly coloured petals (the corolla) and green sepals (the calyx). The prolific Belgian novelist Amélie Nothomb aptly defines a flower as 'a giant sexual organ in its Sunday best'.

Why in the world would anyone eat flowers? It is a given that we eat to survive, but we also eat for pleasure and thus we eat with our eyes and nose as well as our tastebuds. Adding flowers to any cuisine appeals to our senses. We find the shape and colour of flowers pleasing to the eye, their fragrances pleasing to the nose and their taste pleasing to the palate.

While we might not all be aware of it, no doubt the most common edible flowers are broccoli, cauliflower and Brussels sprouts, beautiful vegetables that are actually the flowering portions of the plants. For most vegetables, the fruits or the leaves are eaten, but in the case of these three it is actually the flowering heads that are consumed. Flowers are not typically found in everyday meals, so their deliberate inclusion in a dish makes that dish something special, a treat for the receiver. They send a message of freshness and of caring. In some cultures, specific flowers are ritually used to mark festivals and special occasions. In this way, their appearance in a dish elevates it to something beyond the ordinary. There can also be a health benefit to eating flowers. Since early times, traditional healers have studied the medicinal properties of a wide range of flowers, many of which are still found today in herbal remedies and supplements.

Of course, flowers are seasonal like many other plants and, therefore, short-lived. As a result, the cultivation, distribution and eventual cooking of edible flowers is an expensive proposition, and usually available only to the more affluent. In the Middle Ages, sumptuary laws were created, according to *Black's Law Dictionary*, 'for the purpose of restraining luxury or extravagance, particularly against inordinate expenditures in the matter of apparel, food, furniture, etc.'. Such laws served to reinforce and maintain the social hierarchy. Even today edible flower dishes are more likely to be found in fashionable, high-end restaurants than in a local neighbourhood eatery. Nevertheless, edible flowers are beginning to find favour with a broader spectrum of consumers. For instance,

A simple and easy way to use edible flowers, such as marigolds and nasturtiums, is to garnish devilled eggs.

it is quite possible in the u.s. to find chopped marigolds sprinkled over devilled eggs at a community Fourth of July picnic.

Edible flowers have many culinary uses. Sought after for their flavours, aromas, textures and colours, edible flowers are used fresh, frozen, dried, crystallized or as a foam – in molecular gastronomy – and appear in meat and fish dishes, pastas, salads, soups and desserts. Some common forms of edible flowers are found in garnishes, candied sweets, confits and jellies, pickled flowers or flower vinegars; flavourings such as essences and spice blends; food dyes and colourings; teas, infusions and tisanes; flavoured waters and syrups; and liquors, cordials, bitters, wine, beer and mead.

This book seeks to expand the historical and geographic scope of the already existing work on edible flowers. Divided into geographic regions, the book introduces new floral ingredients and new uses of edible flowers – information we obtained by tapping into immigrant communities and ethnic markets and through our extensive research in many countries. We describe how edible flowers were used historically all around the world from ancient times to today, and explore the new trends in edible flower cuisine that are now unfolding.

It is our hope that this book will encourage readers to explore new flavours and food presentations and enhance our readers' cooking by using edible flowers. Cooking with edible flowers may be easier than you might think, because packagers have already done much of the work for you and have made edible flower products accessible in easy-to-use forms. Furthermore, 'do-it-yourself' readers will find many examples of edible flowers that can easily be cultivated in ordinary gardens.

Li Mengze is a food critic who has written several books about Chinese cuisine in Yunnan Province. In the 26 June 2014 edition of the English-language Chinese newspaper *Global Times*, he sums up our purpose when he writes: 'There has never been a better time to climb aboard the floral cuisine bandwagon. More importantly, the culture behind the passing on of tradition is that people want to become more beautiful and stronger by eating flowers.'

I

The Ancient World

One hundred million years ago, flowers first appeared on earth, carpeting the land with a splendid profusion of shapes, colours and fragrances. By carefully studying how insects and animals interacted with flowers, our earliest ancestors learned which flowers could heal you, which could kill you and which flowers could be sources of food.

Sometime in that misty past humans discovered that flowers were not only beautiful, but that they had many practical uses. The attractive features of flowers, such as their bright colours and fragrances, acted as signposts and even billboards for the location of future sources of food. Their stigmas and stamens, roots and stems, buds and petals could be rendered into traditional medicines and dyes. But an extra bonus was the discovery that a surprisingly large number of flowers were edible. While we cannot accurately pinpoint the exact moment in time when humans first began to eat flowers, we do know that by the time some of the world's ancient civilizations began to flourish, a wide variety of flowers had already been used as medicines and were also important ingredients in cuisine.

Many ancient texts refer to edible flowers. For example, the Bible lists dandelions as one of the 'bitter herbs' eaten as a salad with the Paschal lamb and unleavened bread at

the Hebrew holy day of Passover. The Song of Solomon
(4:13–15) mentions saffron (the stamens of *Crocus sativus*):

> Thy plants are an orchard of pomegranates, with pleasant
> fruits; camphire, with spikenard,
>> Spikenard and saffron; calamus and cinnamon, with
> all trees of frankincense; myrrh and aloes, with all the
> chief spices;
>> A fountain of gardens, a well of living waters, and
> streams from Lebanon.

Moreover, there is an interesting reference to eating flowers
recorded in the apocryphal gospel 4 Esdras 9:23–5, which
reads:

> But if you will let seven days more pass – do not fast
> during them, however; but go into a field of flowers
> where no house has been built, and eat only of the
> flowers of the field, and taste no meat and drink no
> wine, but eat only flowers, and pray to the Most High
> continually – then I will come and talk with you.

Although the Bible only mentions it once, some of
the oldest recorded histories of edible flowers are about
saffron, attesting to the flower's popularity as a colouring
agent, item of medicine and culinary ingredient. A Sumerian
herbal from about 2500 BCE mentions the practice of growing crocus flowers for their prized stamens. Assyrian tablets
dated from 668–626 BCE include saffron among the list of
250 herbal plants. The Sumerians often included saffron
in their medicinals, but they also believed that the smell
and taste were addictive and that too much could kill the
patient.

Another ancient source is the Ebers Papyrus, an Egyptian document dating to 1550 BCE, which contains references to other texts, now lost, dating back another 500 to 2,000 years. The Ebers Papyrus, while primarily a medical text, records how ancient Egyptians cultivated the crocus flower in the royal gardens at Luxor for saffron that was then used in elixirs and potions for temple rituals. Interestingly, the Papyrus also mentions lotus flowers and water lilies being cultivated in the gardens, not only for use in the kitchen, but as food offerings for dead kings in the afterlife.

It is believed that saffron crocuses were first cultivated in Persia, but there is also documentation of the flower being grown in ancient Greece and other Mediterranean cultures

This fragment from the tomb of Nebamun, 1400 BCE, depicts an Egyptian garden surrounded by various plants, including edible flowers.

for thousands of years. The Greeks, in particular, knew well the qualities of saffron and it is from the Greek word *krokus* that we derive the modern term 'crocus'. Images of saffron gatherers appear on Minoan artefacts, such as pottery and in frescoes: the fresco image found in the Minoan Bronze Age ruins at Akrotiri on the island of Santorini dates back to 1500 BCE.

In addition to saffron, ancient Greeks cultivated and ate other flowers, including artichoke, poppy, carnation and lotus. During the wanderings of Odysseus and his crew in Homer's *Odyssey*, the voyagers' ship is blown off course to an unknown land. When Odysseus sends out scouts to explore, they encounter the Lotus-eaters. According to Odysseus:

> it never entered the heads of these natives to kill my friends; what they did was to give them some lotus to taste, and as soon as each had eaten the honeyed fruit of the plant, all thoughts of reporting to us or escaping were banished from his mind. All they now wished for was to stay where they were with the Lotus-eaters, to browse on the lotus, and to forget that they had a home to return to.

It is unclear which lotus Homer actually wrote about and there are several candidates, including *Trifolium*, fellbloom, persimmon, nettle tree and water lily. Recent discoveries reveal that the Egyptians cultivated a blue water lily, also known as blue lotus, that had both soporific and psychotropic qualities.

One of the most interesting ancient texts to mention edible flowers comes to us from Rome. Generally attributed to the first-century CE Roman gastronome and lover of luxury Marcus Gavius Apicius, *Cookery and Dining in Imperial Rome* is

Saffron harvester, Minoan fresco from Santorini, 1600–1500 BCE.

a collection of Roman recipes designed to be used in the kitchen. As such it is one of the world's earliest cookbooks. Its true authorship remains a mystery, however, as the recipes were not compiled until sometime in the fourth or fifth century CE. Whether or not Apicius was truly the author of the book, it remains a fascinating and revealing account of imperial Roman cuisine and cooking. In it Apicius cites recipes that include nasturtium, fennel blossoms and saffron, which are listed as essential spices 'which should be in the house on hand so that there may be nothing wanting'. It also contains recipes for Roman vermouth, which contains saffron, rose and violet wines, rose pie and rose custard, and a 'boiled dinner' that contains capers. A surprisingly modern-sounding recipe for fried frogs' legs includes a fennel flower garnish.

The ancient Romans also used calendula (*Calendula officinalis*), also known as pot marigold, in a variety of ways. It was thought that eating calendula could cause a number of side effects, such as endowing the eater with the power to see fairies, afflicting the eater with sleepiness or making them feel more amorous – although the last two would seem to be contradictory. Calendula could be mixed with vinegar and used in salads and preserves or for seasoning meat. Soups could be flavoured with the dried flower heads and the flowers served as the original dye in cheeses or were used for colouring butter.

Lawrence Alma-Tadema, *The Roses of Heliogabalus*, 1888. Legend has it that the Roman emperor Heliogabalus lured his adversaries to a banquet at which he smothered them with roses.

As the Greeks had before them, Romans used pink and carnation petals in several dishes, calling carnations 'Jove's flower', in honour of one of their beloved gods. Rose petals were used as a flavouring agent not only in Rome, but in Greece, Egypt and Persia. The petals were also eaten as a garnish and candied.

Many of the edible flowers in use among Mediterranean cultures had their origins far to the east and were introduced to the region through trade on the overland Silk Road or through sea-lanes that connected with India through the *Mare Erythraeum*, the classical Latin name for what is today known as the Arabian Sea. In addition to spices such as anise, cinnamon, nutmeg and pepper, these trade routes also brought in edible flowers that included cloves – with the Phoenicians controlling much of that business – and roses, which appear to have been originally cultivated both in Persia and China.

Asia

Since Neolithic times, edible flowers such as daylilies and chrysanthemums have been popular in China, while the lotus has been a beloved flower because it is believed to balance food choices and to extend a person's longevity. Ancient lotus recipes have been found written on bamboo slips and pieces of silk. Lotus petals were eaten raw or battered and fried, the dried stamens were brewed into a tea and nearly every other part of the lotus plant found its way into ancient Chinese cuisine. The plant is still used today in a myriad of modern Chinese dishes.

Rose cultivation can be traced back to China's Shennong Dynasty (*c.* 2737–2697 BCE). Prized for their beauty and fragrance, roses also found their way into wine, and rose wine remains a popular ingredient in Chinese barbecue and sauces today. Chinese herbs, including flowers, have been used as medicine as well as food for centuries. According to Chinese mythology, Shennong, sometimes called the 'God of Chinese herbal medicine', catalogued 365 species of medicinal plants, but died when he ate a flower he did not know was toxic. In the Chinese tradition, jasmine is believed to reduce internal heat and calm the nerves. Among the earliest literature are lists of prescriptions detailed in the *Recipes for 52 Ailments*, found in the Mawangdui tombs which were sealed in 168 BCE.

As long as 2,500 years ago, Chinese traders brought cloves from Ternate, also called Clove Island, which is one of the Molucca Islands. Cloves eventually found their way to the Middle East where Arab traders in turn introduced them to Europe during the days of the Roman Empire.

The Nung Din people of Lao Cai in northern Vietnam make an unusual rice dish called *xoi bay mau*, commonly known as 'seven-colour rice'. As the name implies, local flowers and other ingredients are used to dye the rice in seven different and vibrant hues such as scarlet, bright green, yellow and purple, among others. The dish has been made for centuries and dates back to a time when the Nung Din people expelled the Chinese Han invaders who had seized their lands. The war lasted for seven months and each colour symbolically represents one of those months. Making the dish is a laborious process and so it is a special treat typically reserved for festival celebrations.

In India, the use of edible flowers, especially for their colour and fragrance, is an important part of the practice of Ayurveda. Translated from Sanskrit, Ayurveda, which means 'life knowledge', is a system of Hindu traditional medicine with origins as early as 1500 BCE in the Indus Valley. As in

Chinese food theories, various flowers are considered 'hot' or 'cold'; creating balance in our behaviour or our physical body is the goal. One of the earliest records of edible flowers in India is found in the popular ancient Sanskrit epic poem the *Ramayana*. When the hero Rama and his wife Sita are exiled into the forest, they are aided by the wise Agastya who serves

Seven-coloured rice, a speciality of tribal groups in Sapa, in the northern mountains of Vietnam.

Rama and his wife Sita being fed a 'supper of edible flowers and bulbs' by Agastya, from the Sanskrit epic *Ramayana*, 1649, painting from the Mewar Ramayana Manuscript.

the couple a 'supper of edible flowers and bulbs that left them with not the slightest thought of hunger'.

The Americas

In the Americas, the record of indigenous people consuming flowers goes back almost 5,000 years. When Spanish *conquistadores* came to the New World they called any unknown large and colourful flower a 'rose'. The Aztecs, however, had already developed an entire lexicon for flowers based upon their own usage. The Aztec word for an edible flower was *quilitl*.

It would be an understatement to say that the Aztecs liked flowers; they loved them. The Dominican friar Diego Durán (1537–1588) wrote:

They become the happiest people in the world smelling them, for these natives in general are most sensuous and pleasure loving. They find goodness and joy in spending the entire day smelling a little flower or a bouquet made of different kinds of flowers; their gifts are accompanied by them; they relieve the tediousness of journeys with flowers. To sum up, they find the smelling of flowers so comforting that they even stave off and manage to survive hunger by smelling them.

Not only did the Aztecs halt hunger by smelling the flowers, but by eating them as well. Throughout the Americas indigenous peoples found the flowers of various pumpkins and squashes to be edible, either fresh or stuffed with other ingredients and fried. In Central America the flowers of yucca plants and the century plant (*Agave americana*) were also eaten.

In South America, the Incas of Peru cultivated two varieties of nasturtium, which they used both as a medicinal herb and in salads. These flowers would later be transported to Europe by Spanish *conquistadores*, becoming the original stock for most of the nasturtiums we know today. Although considered more of a tropical flower, a variety of the genus *Hibiscus* also grows in the Andes, where indigenous peoples found they could eat the petals raw, although they had a slightly acidic taste. A better use for hibiscus petals was to put them in *mate*, a traditional South American caffeine-rich drink particularly favoured in Argentina.

Cacao was considered a sacred drink throughout Central and South America and was frequently flavoured with various flowers, such as marigold or heart flower (*Magnolia mexicana*), a favourite of the Maya. In North America, indigenous people found ways to use cattails and red clover in their dishes. Bee balm was also frequently brewed into a tea for medicinal purposes.

All around the globe, on every inhabited continent, people discovered early on the value of flowers as a food source. As science, technology, agricultural methods and trade advanced over the centuries, new and creative ways have been discovered in which to include flowers in global cuisines.

2
The Middle Ages to the Nineteenth Century

The history of edible flowers in Europe and the Middle East is extensive and diverse. When the barbarians overthrew the last Roman emperor, Romulus Augustulus, in 476 CE, the old Roman Empire was dead. The Byzantine Empire, however, centred in Constantinople, continued to thrive in the East. Fortunately, much of the accumulated knowledge of that vast Byzantine Empire survived and was preserved over the following centuries in monasteries, including much valuable information about plants and flowers.

During the Middle Ages, monks throughout Europe carefully cultivated medicinal plants in monastery gardens and developed extensive pharmacopoeias. Of the 160 medicinal plants Robin Whitemen cites in *Brother Cadfael's Herb Garden: An Illustrated Companion to Medieval Plants and their Uses* (1997), 24 were herbal flowers. These gardens included flowers that had been known to the ancients as possessing medicinal powers, flowers such as primrose and calendula, which the monks called 'pot marigold' because of its ubiquitous use in their soup pots. Chamomile, an age-old medicinal herb known in Egypt, Greece and Rome, became ever more popular during the Middle Ages as a remedy for a plethora of ailments including asthma, colic, fever, inflammation, nausea, nervous conditions, skin diseases and cancer, not to mention the plague.

Upper Rhenish Master, *Little Garden of Paradise*, c. 1410–c. 1420, tempera on wood. Medieval gardens of the rich and powerful members of society preserved and cultivated edible flowers. Although edible, they were grown primarily for medicinal use.

The Middle Ages saw a growth in trade throughout Europe and the beginning of the rise of a commercial middle class. One little flower, hops (*Humulus lupulus*), discovered and cultivated by monks in their carefully tended gardens, played a part in this story; the monks' discovery of the power of these flowers still pleases us today. Wild hops had been consumed for centuries before the monks began growing them; Roman soldiers ate them and Hildegard of Bingen wrote about the medicinal properties of hop oils.

According to Evan D. G. Fraser and Andrew Rimas in their book *Empires of Food* (2010), when monks discovered that adding hops to beer during the fermentation process provided an antimicrobial element that ensured the beer would last much longer – for several months if properly stored – they realized that they had created a commodity that could be transported and traded far and wide without spoiling. The monasteries lost no time in becoming profitable breweries. William the Conqueror's Domesday Book from 1086 records the monks of St Paul's Cathedral in London brewing nearly 80,000 gallons of beer annually. The booming trade in beer, begun by the monks, resulted in the increase in demand for the trading of other foods. This, in turn, helped to create the rise of market towns throughout Europe.

Another flower that influenced world trade and improved cultural exchange between nations was the clove, the aromatic flower buds of a tree in the family Myrtaceae, which are native to the Molucca Islands in Indonesia. Cloves reached the Roman Empire through a trade route that originated in the East Indies and progressed through India, terminating at the Persian Gulf or Red Sea. At that time, however, the dried flower buds were more commonly used as perfume or incense. By the Middle Ages cloves were also found in spice mixtures in Europe, the Middle East and Asia. In the ninth century monks at the St Gall monastery in Switzerland spiced their fasting fish with cloves, and an Arab traveller in the tenth century reported seeing the burghers of Mainz, Germany, seasoning their dishes with cloves. Crusading Frankish knights spiced their food with cloves, although it is not known if they did so because of the popular belief that drinking sweet milk containing three grams of crushed cloves could restore a man's potency. Throughout the Middle East and Asia, cloves could be found as the one common ingredient in a variety of five-spices mixtures. *Poudre fine*, which translates literally as 'excellent powder', was another spice mix of the Middle Ages that contained cloves as a prime ingredient. Cloves were also a major component of Four

Thieves Vinegar, a concoction believed to help ward off the Black Death.

Monks used flowering herbs not only to cure medical complaints but to prevent them from occurring in the first place, so the inclusion of various flowers in monastic meals became common. A method of determining which flowers would be beneficial to counter a particular ailment was known as the 'doctrine of signatures'. It relied upon matching the physical characteristics of the plant with the medical condition in question. As an example, cowslip, with its trembling, nodding flowers, was believed to be a cure for palsy, because of the identical symptoms exhibited by the patients in their extremities and heads.

As the flowers and flowering herbs that had been grown by the monks for medicinal purposes gained popularity outside monastic walls, aristocratic and affluent merchant families began to plant them in their own gardens. *The Goodman of Paris*, written in 1393 by a wealthy burgher to his new wife forty years his junior, is a detailed guide that explains how a wife should manage her household. It has practical advice on gardening and cooking and illustrates, in part, how the cultivation of plants and flowers for culinary purposes had spread from the cloistered gardens of the monasteries to the personal gardens of people of means.

This new, rising merchant class recognized the medicinal value of plants but they also prized their sensory qualities: their colours, fragrances, shapes and even their flavours. A new appreciation for these flowers developed as people began to recognize their aesthetic appeal alongside their culinary importance. Rose, orange and jasmine flower waters were used to perfume food, while saffron imparted a rich, golden colour to the dishes of those who could afford the expensive flower. Among the wealthy, saffron could be found sparkling in dishes

'A Figure of the Five Islands Where Grow the Cloves, and of Their Tree', from vol. II of *Magellan's Voyage: A Narrative Account of the First Circumnavigation* by Antonio Pigafetta (1521).

Peasant picking saffron, from the 14th-century *Tacuinum sanitatis*, a health handbook from the Middle Ages.

to imitate gold. Indeed, saffron could be just as costly as gold itself. In *Eating Right in the Renaissance* (2002), Ken Albala writes:

> There are some striking parallels between art history and culinary history especially concerning the use of gold. It may be no coincidence that gold backgrounds [in paintings] and gold-coloured foods both go out of fashion at roughly the same time, somewhere in the early sixteenth century.

The art of distillation, perfected by the Arabs – and, in particular, credited to the tenth-century Arab physician Avicenna, who is largely believed to have discovered the distillation process – allowed the essence of some flowers to be captured in 'waters', such as rosewater and orange blossom water. Rosewater was a favourite ingredient in the dishes of many countries, especially those of Persia and the Middle East. The Persians had already been using rose petals in their cooking, both for fragrance and taste, before rosewater was invented. Crusaders returning home to Europe brought with

Floral distilling equipment.

them roses and rosewater. Blancmange, a British dessert, which originally in both France and England was frequently flavoured with rosewater, was invented by the Arabs but spread throughout Europe in the medieval period – a version was being made in France in the thirteenth century and the Cook in Chaucer's *The Canterbury Tales* talks about making it.

In the Middle East, *Kitab al-Tabikh* (A Baghdad Cookery Book), composed by a thirteenth-century scribe named al-Baghdadi and translated into English by A. J. Arberry in 1939, contained recipes that date as far back as the ninth century. The book includes many recipes for meats and stews and almost all of them instruct the cook to sprinkle the pot with rosewater as a final step. Other recipes suggest colouring the food with saffron.

According to the Qur'an, all of God's creations are good and good Muslims should enjoy them. With this directive, medieval Arab cooks worked to make their cuisine as beautiful, exciting and delicious as possible, especially since food was considered the greatest of all pleasures, even above riches, drink and sex. A common spice mixture designed to stimulate the senses of sight, smell and taste was called *atraf al-tib*. It contained, among other ingredients, lavender, cloves and rosebuds.

There are at least two sweet dishes containing edible flowers mentioned in *One Thousand and One Nights*, a collection of Middle Eastern and South Asian stories and folk tales compiled in Arabic sometime during the ninth or tenth century. *Kadayif* was a small yeast griddle cake with a rubbery texture, stuffed with nuts and soaked in syrup flavoured with rosewater, and this cake later evolved into a shredded pastry drenched in rosewater syrup. *Zerde* was a rice pudding coloured with saffron and flavoured with rosewater, orange-flower water or rose geranium.

The Ottoman Empire spanned an extensive region around the Mediterranean from 1453 to 1923. Rosewater and rose flavouring were very popular in both sweet and savoury dishes in Ottoman palace cuisine. Reviewing meticulous records of palace expenses, it is possible to list almost every sherbet made of floral ingredients in the confectionery of the Topkapı Palace, including violet, *gül maa gülşeker* (rose and sugar flavoured with rose), rose and lemon, red rose, water lily and narcissus.

The rise of humanist philosophy in the Renaissance period positioned food as a pleasure rather than as a temptation to gluttony and lust, an attitude often found in medieval thought. As a result, flowers became more frequent ingredients in the culinary repertoires of chefs throughout Europe and the Middle East. In his book *Da Vinci's Kitchen* (2006), Dave Dewitt mentions that even Leonardo da Vinci had a cookbook in his personal library: Platina's *On Right Pleasure and Good Health*. The book contains hundreds of recipes that include rosewater, saffron, cloves, elderberry flowers and fennel flowers, as well as other flowers; a recipe for 'apple tart in the French style' sounds like an ancestor to American apple pie but flavoured with rosewater.

In fifteenth-century England, mixed herb and flower salads containing borage, daisies, primrose and violets became common and desserts included cakes made with rosewater or elderflower vinegar. Conserves were made from sage flowers, peonies and lavender, although such conserves were used more as a medicinal tonic than a culinary addition. Even the country's poor were consuming flowers such as bee balm, borage, chrysanthemums, daylilies, nasturtiums, pot marigolds, roses and violets.

As European powers vied for new trade routes, especially for spices, in the fifteenth century, new fauna and flora were discovered on traders' travels and brought back to Europe. With the colonization of the Americas and European outposts being established in Asia and Africa, the two-way cultivation of plants – among them edible flowers – flourished. The Spanish were the first to introduce New World plants to Europe, but other countries such as England, France, the Dutch republic and Portugal soon followed suit.

John Gerard was a plant expert and superintendent of the gardens of William Cecil, an advisor to Elizabeth I. These gardens contained New World plants, which he added to a book which became commonly known as Gerard's *Herball*, although it was largely an English translation of a book originally written by the Flemish botanist Rembert Dodoens in 1554. By the time Gerard's book was first published in 1597, flowers had already become important ingredients in English dishes. But, like the monks of the Middle Ages, Gerard had great respect for the medicinal quality of flowers and warned that potently flavoured mixtures must be used with caution, especially when administered by 'unlearned physicians and diverse rash and overbold apothecaries, and other foolish women'.

Nicholas Culpeper's *Complete Herbal*, published in England in 1653, was, similar to Gerard's book, a compendium of pharmaceutical and herbal knowledge. Culpeper was an apothecary, botanist, herbalist, physician and astrologer. It is that last vocation that influences the scientific credibility of his book, causing some people to denigrate its value. Still, Culpeper was a keen observer of the medicinal qualities of plants. Of the white dead nettle, also known as the white archangel, he wrote: 'Flowers of the white archangel are preserved or conserved to be used to stay the whites, and the flowers of the red to stay the reds in women. It makes the head merry, drives away melancholy, quickens the spirits.'

The title page of John Gerard's *Herball* (1597).

Banquet scene from the Tang Dynasty (618–907 CE), during which edible flowers reached their zenith in China.

In 1747 Hannah Glasse published her immodestly titled cookbook, *The Art of Cookery, made Plain and Easy, Which far exceeds any Thing of the Kind ever yet Published*. Glasse's book was wildly popular in England during the Georgian period. It was almost entirely derivative, as she simply lifted recipes from other books and compiled them in her own work, but what set her book apart from the others was the audience for whom it was written. Her book was not intended for ladies of the household, as were other cookbooks of the times, but rather were written for, in Glasse's words, 'the lower sort' – literate domestic servants. Many of her recipes employed edible flowers, including one for 'cordial poppy water' that required 2 gallons of brandy and 'a peck of poppies'.

During the so-called 'Dark Ages' in Europe, China was experiencing a golden age of trade during the Tang Dynasty

Banquet miniature, from the 16th-century memoirs of Babur. During the extravagant and luxurious reign of the Mughals in India, edible flowers flavoured many dishes, such as *gulab jamun*, a dessert made with rose-flavoured syrup.

(618–907). The popularity of edible flowers reached its height during this time, when women started to consume flowers for their cosmetic properties in order to improve their complexions. Wu Zetian, China's only female emperor (r. 690–705), is reputed to have been responsible for creating *bai hu gao* (hundred flower cake), and was also said to enjoy cookies that included 'piney flowers'.

One of the earliest surviving Chinese-language cookbooks is Hu Sihui's *Yinshan Zhengyao* (Important Principles of Food and Drink), believed to be from 1330. Hu Sihui was a dietitian to the Mongol ruler, Buyantu Khan, and his book shows how the Chinese were influenced by Central Asian cuisine eaten by members of the Yuan court. The book's recipes were adapted from foods eaten all over the Mongol Empire.

In India, the Mughal Empire flourished from 1526 to 1707, although it lasted longer in a diminished capacity until the time of the nineteenth-century British Raj. The Mughals brought a flowering of art, culture and government to the Indian subcontinent and were known for their lavish lifestyles and appreciation for all sensual delights, including food. During this period, Iranian and Central Asian culinary traditions combined with the native Indian cuisine to create a whole new range of taste sensations and cooking delights, of which edible flowers were very much a part. Two desserts from that period have their roots in Persian cuisine: *luqmat al-qadi* was an Arab dessert that used rosewater syrup and sometimes saffron syrup along with honey; and it is believed that *gulab jamun*, one of India's most popular desserts, derived from it. The latter dessert combines dumplings made from milk soaked in rose-flavoured sugar water. It can be eaten plain or topped with ice cream and it is often served at Indian celebrations and festivals.

3
The Victorian Era to Today

During the Victorian period (1837–1901), particularly in Britain, flowers were very much a part of the everyday aesthetic, from floral-printed fabrics and porcelain dinnerware to virtual forests of floral centrepieces on tabletops. Victorians developed a complex 'language of flowers' and the sheer romance of flower-encrusted sweets, pastries and salads delighted them. Candied flowers were particularly popular since the process not only preserved the delicate blooms but added texture and sweetness.

In her book *The Scented Kitchen: Cooking with Flowers* (2007), Frances Bissell points out that there is actually surprisingly little evidence of the use of flowers as a culinary ingredient in the recipes found in the cookbooks of Victorian cooking stars, such as Miss Acton (*Modern Cookery for Private Families*, 1845), Mrs Beeton (*Household Management*, 1861) and Mrs Marshall (*Book of Cookery*, 1888). However, Mrs Marshall, nicknamed 'Queen of the Ices' for her numerous ice cream recipes, did include rosewater ice, jasmine ice water and an orange water ice cream in her book *Ices Plain and Fancy: The Book of Ices* (1885). Bissell also notes that studying household recipe books in country archives does not reveal an extensive culinary usage of floral ingredients other than saffron and cloves.

Candied flowers and floral-themed postcards show the importance of flowers to the Victorians.

Although commonly thought of as a morally restrained period, the Victorian era was romantic and adventurous, embracing democracy, women's rights and workers' rights. So, these modern women were writing for the female heads of households, women who no longer had servants to prepare elaborate culinary concoctions. One woman, however, who did have access to abundant help at about the same period in China was the Empress Dowager Cixi (1835–1908), who presided over grand imperial banquets and was said to have enjoyed lotus-petal fritters. In the ancient imperial court of the Nguyen Dynasty in Vietnam (1802–1945), Emperor Tu

Duc had enough servants that he could demand that a handful of tea be put into one of the lotus flowers blooming in a lake on the palace grounds, and for it to then be retrieved in the morning and used to make the most elegant flower tea.

Meanwhile, back in Europe and America, the ascendancy of the Industrial Revolution clashed with the aesthetic inclinations of the Victorians, marking a major turning point in almost every aspect of daily life, including food preparation; cooking with flowers virtually disappeared. Transportation of food ingredients, and important changes and advances in agricultural production, meant that food became more readily available to the increasing number of urban dwellers who had little or no access to gardens for producing their own fresh food.

Lydia Pinkham's Herbal Liquid Supplement contains dandelion and continues to be marketed today.

Vanilla, which had become easily imported and therefore readily available and inexpensive, replaced rosewater as one of the most commonly used floral ingredients. New advances in food technology meant that food could be canned, frozen or stored in jars, thereby lasting longer and effectively eliminating the seasonality of garden produce. While these developments in food preservation were beneficial for the production and storage of vegetables, they certainly did not work for delicate, edible flowers, which were not easy to transport, inspect or label. As a result, the use of edible flowers severely declined.

The u.s. Federal Food, Drug and Cosmetic Act of 1938 prohibited false therapeutic claims and required all products covered under the act to comply with new consumer safety standards. The act effectively put an end to the sale of dubious 'snake-oil' elixirs, which frequently contained edible flowers. Even though the public came to trust synthetic pharmaceuticals more than homegrown remedies, some of the earlier elixirs survived, rebranding themselves as herbal supplements or homeopathic medicines. Bach Flower Remedies, still available today, were developed in the 1930s by Edward Bach, an English homeopath, who – because of his perceived psychic connections with flower 'essences' – believed in the healing power of the dew found on flower petals. Also still in distribution is Lydia Pinkham's 'Vegetable Compound for Female Weaknesses', containing dandelion and originally marketed in the late 1900s. Nicknamed 'Lily the Pink', Pinkham is described in an old drinking song as a 'shrewd operator' whom many modern-day feminists admire for distributing information about menstruation and the 'facts of life'.

The evolution of the modern pharmaceutical industry in the United States and other developed nations changed people's perceptions of medicine. People learned to trust labels and government assurances of content and safety over oral history and traditional folk knowledge, ushering in what could be called the 'dark ages' of edible flowers. Still, throughout the rest of the world, European Roma, indigenous peoples and traditional healers continue to keep the knowledge of medicinal flowers alive.

The War Years

During the First and Second World Wars, and the interwar economic depression, food was at a premium and luxury foods practically disappeared. This included edible flowers, except for the familiar staple vegetables that are actually flowers, such as cauliflower and broccoli. Nevertheless, there were notable champions of floral cookery to be found during this period. Mrs C. F. Lyle, author of *The Gentle Art of Cookery with 750 Recipes*, first published in 1925, included a chapter entitled 'Flower Recipes' with instructions for a wide range of flower dishes from chrysanthemum salad to rose ice cream. Having considerable knowledge of the use of herbs and spices, Mrs Lyle noted in her introduction that her book had been 'written for those who appreciate the fact that good cooking is one of the attainable amenities of life if extravagance is eliminated', as it is during wars and economic depression. In 1926 Mrs Lyle wrote *The Magic of Herbs* and a year later opened Culpeper House in London to sell herbal remedies, cosmetics and food.

Victory gardens (also called war gardens) emerged on the home fronts during these conflicts as a way of minimizing demand on an overburdened public food system, and they allowed citizens to feel that they were supporting the war effort. Citizens were encouraged to grow their own fruit and vegetables so that more of the foods coming out of the mass-processing facilities could be shipped overseas to soldiers. A garden diagram from the First World War shows calendulas and pot marigolds as edible flowers to be cultivated. Home gardens are once again becoming popular, but this time the goal is different. The emphasis now is on growing your own food so that you have control over how it is grown and how much you pay for it.

Not all edible flower experiences were positive. In the winter of 1944–5, as the Second World War was drawing to a close, a great famine swept through the Netherlands, forcing the people to eat tulip bulbs. Many citizens of a certain age remember the famine and the tulip bulbs they ate. Antoinette van Heugten in *The Tulip Eaters* (2013) quotes a Dutch housewife in *c.* 1944:

> We have no milk, no bread, no potatoes – just rotten peels. The boys now have to go far into the fields to pull frozen tulip bulbs from the ground. We grind the pulp and make thin soup and water porridges from them. They are bitter, practically inedible, but we choke them down because otherwise we will starve.

Amid the widespread wartime deprivation during the twentieth century, there were some rare examples of the luxury and beauty that flowers can bring to cuisine. As the Second World War German occupation came to an end in Paris, Alice B. Toklas, the companion of Gertrude Stein, published her famous cookbook, which included a '14th of July Salad' that was made with capers and nasturtiums, and 'Liberation Fruit Cake' with cloves and rose- and orange-flower water, which Toklas and Stein served to American officers. The British floral designer to the rich and famous,

Alice B. Toklas (left) and Gertrude Stein entertained with edible flowers.

Constance Spry, turned her hand to writing cookbooks during the Second World War. In *Come into the Garden, Cook*, Spry suggests ways to use the old-fashioned heirloom roses that she had previously promoted in her spectacular arrangements in austerity cooking.

In other parts of the world, people would sometimes turn to edible flowers in troubled times. For instance, the cork flower, which is also called the katary flower, is the flower of the corkwood tree and is found in Indonesia, the Philippines and Malaysia. The flower is either light burgundy or white in colour and was eaten raw, possibly as a last resort in times of famine. It is still often eaten uncooked, despite its bitter, astringent taste, but can also be sautéed or made into a soup or a type of porridge. In Vietnam, the *dien dien* flower blooms with yellow flowers about a month after the yearly floods in the Mekong delta. The flowers provide a source of food for the farmers during what can be a time of severe hunger. The flowers were typically served with linh fish or combined into snakehead-fish sour soup.

Modern Times

The victory garden movement generally lost momentum when the troops came home in 1945, at least partly because people associated victory gardens with hard times. In the 1950s women entered the workplace in large numbers. At the same time their roles as homemakers were made easier by modern kitchen appliances, convenience foods such as TV dinners and packaged foods, and the rise of fast-food restaurants. All of this resulted in the decline of kitchen gardens and the almost complete elimination of culinary flowers.

The rebellious 1960s, with its hippie counterculture and 'flower children', sparked a return-to-the-land movement that valued all things natural and organic. The publication of Rachel Carson's *Silent Spring* in 1962 brought public awareness to the devastating effects of pesticides and other toxins upon the environment and helped create a renewed interest in organic gardening. As a result, edible flowers once again became objects of interest. Foraging the woods and fields of America for edible flowers, plants and nuts became an offbeat but increasingly popular pastime, and foraging enthusiasts like Euell Gibbons became national celebrities.

Another culinary phenomenon of the 1960s was a new appreciation for fine European – especially French – cuisine, but this time with a decidedly democratic twist. Julia Child's *Mastering the Art of French Cooking* (1961) and her light-hearted television cooking show took the snobbery and sense of superiority out of European cuisine and showed America and the world that anyone could prepare fine meals. Since edible flowers had continued to be used by the grand chefs of haute cuisine, they now found a place in the repertoire of more modest cooks and chefs.

In Europe during this time, French chefs began experimenting with a new approach to cooking and food presentation called *nouvelle cuisine*, which favoured lighter, more delicate dishes and an increased emphasis on presentation. Edible flowers featured prominently in *nouvelle cuisine* dishes both as garnishes and as food items in their own right. In addition, flowers added to a dish enhanced the perception of freshness, an important concept in *nouvelle cuisine*.

In 1964 Alice Waters, a renowned chef from Berkeley, California, made her memorable first trip to France where she was impressed with what was to become the farm-to-table movement, a celebration of fresh and local ingredients.

First Lady Michelle Obama has encouraged Americans to grow neighbourhood gardens. The White House garden includes edible flowers such as marigolds and nasturtiums.

She thereafter championed a cuisine that required the use of the freshest ingredients, used only at the peak of their season and nearly always grown locally and organically. According to Thomas McNamee, writing in *Alice Waters and Chez Panisse* (2008), 'Alice Waters has transformed the way many Americans eat and the way they feel about food.' Throughout her career, the use of flowers has always been integral to the dining experience and, in fact, one of the 'memorable meals' that Waters published in her book, *The Chez Panisse Menu Cookbook*, is a beautiful 'Dinner of Flowers'.

In 1996 Alice Waters founded the Chez Panisse Foundation and created the Edible Schoolyard programme at the Martin Luther King Middle School in Berkeley. She is presently a public policy advocate on the national level for school lunch reform and universal access to healthy, organic foods. The impact of her organic and healthy food revolution is typified by Michelle Obama's White House organic vegetable garden, which also features some edible flowers such as marigolds and nasturtiums. The Edible Schoolyard programme reflects, in part, the inclusion of multiculturalism in the American school curriculum, a process which began in the 1980s. School curricula emphasized understanding, respect and appreciation of different lifestyles and traditions. In terms of food and edible flowers, multiculturalism manifested in the form of ethnic cookbooks and restaurants, ethnic food sections in supermarkets and the proliferation of ethnic markets.

Whether grown in home gardens or commercially cultivated, edible flowers require organic agriculture. Before 1980 the market for organically grown produce, including edible flowers, was small, with fewer than half a dozen natural food supermarkets in the United States selling organic produce. But in 1980 Whole Foods Market, with its emphasis on natural and organic food, opened and became the first organically certified grocer in the United States. Others saw the success of Whole Foods Market and joined in the move toward healthier food, countering the destructive trend toward processed food that had led to a fundamental shift in the United States's agricultural base from locally grown, fresh produce to corn-based fast food that used high-fructose corn syrup as a common ingredient. With this interest in natural and organic foods came a renewed interest in edible flowers; most Whole Foods Market stores feature local edible flowers in their section of fresh herbs. Bee pollen has also found a place on store shelves, in the form of tablets and granules. It has a sweet taste and can be added to granola, cereal or yoghurt, sprinkled on salads or included in smoothies.

The increased appreciation of and interest in other cultures has led to the increased use of edible flowers worldwide and has also created an economic boom for some regions. In China's Yunnan Province, for example, ethnobotanists have identified more than 160 species of edible flowers in the diet of the local ethnic people, who consume flowers as commonly as one would eat vegetables. Traditionally, people in Yunnan utilized roses as food, especially in their flower cakes, which were eaten at breakfast and as snacks. The flower cake has been around for a long time, but mostly as a local speciality. In recent years Yunnan farmers have developed new flower products, such as rose sugar, rose jam, rose lozenges, rose drinks, fresh juices and a rose liqueur. Elsewhere, in West Africa, particularly Senegal and Mali, non-profit organizations and government agencies are assisting local people to cultivate an edible variety of hibiscus. Furthermore, Bob Allen, an American living in Vietnam, and his wife Hue operate Golden Garden in Dalat, where they cultivate speciality greens and edible flowers that are sold to restaurants and markets throughout Vietnam.

The reclamation of edible flowers by modern chefs, often Michelin-starred ones, has given them a new place in modern cuisine. In the 1990s Michel Bras and Marc Veyrat, both three-star French chefs, legitimized the placement of edible flowers on Michelin-starred plates. Ferran Adrià, another pioneer in using edible flowers at his three-star restaurant, El Bulli in Roses, Spain, created paper flower tea soup and elder and borage flower sorbet. Heston Blumenthal, the English celebrity chef and proprietor of The Fat Duck restaurant in England, garnished plates with edible flowers and leaves, creating entire miniature gardens.

The Twenty-first Century

In a *Newsweek* article dated 18 July 2014, the writer Anissa Helou wrote: 'The trend for eating wild – foraging what is fresh and local – has given blooms a new life.' In Copenhagen, Denmark, the world-famous Noma restaurant has been at the forefront of the movement to bring flowers into food. One recent Noma menu featured edible seasonal flowers such as chrysanthemums and roses in every single dish.

In order to better source beautiful, unusual ingredients, including flowers for both garnishes and cooking, several famous restaurants now have professional foragers on their payrolls. Also, chefs are increasingly hiring consultants to help with menu development, including taking edible flowers to a new level. Faviken restaurant in northern Sweden is located within a secluded farming estate; its chef, Magnus Nilsson, cooks with what he finds right outside the kitchen door, and he forages for the prettiest field flowers to use as the top layer in a delicious tartare made of ox-heart and bone marrow. In California, at Meadowood, a three-Michelin-star restaurant in the Napa Valley, Christopher Kostow also picks flowering herbs and seasonal blossoms from his restaurant garden and the surrounding grounds. In addition to using flowers to enhance the aesthetic appeal of the meal, both of these chefs view them as an essential ingredient.

In Helou's *Newsweek* article, the British chef James Lowe, owner of Lyle's in London, describes how he uses flowers in his kitchen: 'The important point about using edible flowers is that they are part of what I think truly seasonal food is.' Lyle continues, 'I like to think that seasonal food means putting what's available outside on the plate.' In addition to professional foragers, and chefs who actually do their own foraging, the number of edible flower cultivators and distributors is expanding. There are many relatively small, local businesses such as Spring Thyme Herbs in Hockesson, Delaware, that specialize in local, seasonal varieties of edible flowers that are sold to local markets, including area Whole Foods Market stores.

There are also some large operations in the edible flower business. Lee Jones, a farmer, and his family run Chef's Garden in Huron, Ohio, a farm that raises microgreens and edible flowers. But Chef's Garden is no rural farm-stand operation. Rather, it is a high-tech, mechanized business in which flowers are harvested, washed, packaged and shipped overnight to customers all around the world, including many high-end restaurants and the Disney Corporation. Farmer Lee maintains a sophisticated quality-control laboratory that ensures the flowers are free of any contaminants and even monitors the quality of the water used to wash the flowers after they are harvested. Farmer Lee scored a major coup when his farm supplied the American team of chefs competing in the 2015 prestigious Bocuse d'Or competition in France with edible flowers for their creations, shipping them overseas by air.

Molecular Gastronomy

Molecular gastronomy is a new and exciting sub-discipline of food science. Chefs working in this specialization resemble the alchemists of old as they seek to understand the physical and chemical transformations of ingredients that occur in cooking. The components of molecular gastronomy include the three important points of cooking: social, artistic and technical.

Edible flowers are finding a place in molecular gastronomy, partly because of the artistic and technical challenges they pose for chefs working with them. The chef Ferran Adrià has developed a technique that consists of trapping begonias, marigolds and herb flowers in candy floss (cotton candy) and compressing the mixture to form an edible paper. The benefit of this technique is that it doesn't require heat and all the flowers still look fresh and bright.

It is not yet clear whether molecular gastronomy is simply a fascinating but ephemeral trend, or whether it is here to stay, but the discipline shows an increasing fascination for the discovery of new ingredients such as edible flowers. Perhaps this simply mirrors an evolving desire by chefs and food lovers alike to experience more new ingredients and new tastes. Either way, it augurs well for the expanding use and acceptance of edible flowers as an important culinary ingredient.

4
Asia

According to Hinduism, one of the world's oldest religions, food is a gift from the gods and should be treated with great respect. Hinduism places such great emphasis on the role of food that it has been called 'the kitchen religion'. No religious or public function is complete without the distribution of food, especially *prasada* (food offered to the gods). According to the Vedic scriptures, all food should be offered as a sacrifice to the gods before it is eaten. This act of offering bestows religious merit and purifies the body, mind and spirit. Both food and flowers are essential components of a *puja*, the Hindu prayer ritual.

Particular flowers and foods are linked to specific deities. For example, the goddess Lakshmi, consort of Vishnu, is thought to be especially fond of offerings of the sweet Roshogolla, made with a rosewater syrup. A popular form of Lord Krishna, an avatar of the god Vishnu, is represented as a chubby toddler, called Laddu Gopal, who favours the ball-shaped sweet *laddu*, which is made with cloves and saffron.

In China, various foods and flowers are particularly enjoyed because they represent happiness, health, luck or prosperity. At each meal, a Chinese diner feels that he adds to his virtue, strengthens his resistance to illness and possibly cures his ailments. At the heart of Chinese culture is the philosophy of yin and yang, balance in all things. How does the concept of yin and yang relate to food? Certain foods, including the many kinds of flowers that are consumed, are thought to have yin or cooling properties, while others have warm, yang properties. The challenge is to consume a diet that contains a healthy balance of the two.

Chrysanthemum

The name 'chrysanthemum' is derived from the Greek words *chrysos* (gold) and *anthemon* (flower), and while there are countless varieties worldwide, most species originate in East Asia. In the yin and yang of Chinese cuisine, chrysanthemum is thought to be 'cool' and eating chrysanthemums is believed to increase longevity. Eating the stems, roots and flowers will supposedly turn white hair black again, make the body vigorous and cause teeth to grow back.

The cultivation of chrysanthemums as a food source in China dates back to about 500 BCE. The base of the petals are bitter, and should be snapped off before eating. They are often floated in soups or sprinkled for colour into other dishes. Not only are the flowers of chrysanthemum important to Chinese cooking, but the foliage of one variety (*Chrysanthemum coronarium*) is also edible. Dried chrysanthemum flower petals are made into tea and the flowers are believed to ease sore throats, reduce fever and cleanse the liver.

Chrysanthemum wine was regarded in ancient times as 'auspicious wine' that people were to drink on the Double Ninth Festival (the ninth day of the ninth month in the Chinese calendar), also called the Chong Yang Festival, to prevent disasters and to pray for blessings. On the Double Ninth

A package of Chinese Five-flower Tea, containing chrysanthemums.

Festival each year, chrysanthemum wine was made to be drunk in the following year. It is said that people who drink it can prolong their life, chrysanthemums having high medicinal value. Chrysanthemum wine was routinely served in the imperial palace during this festival in the reign of Emperor Wu Di of the Han Dynasty (206 BCE–220 CE).

The American cookbook writer Craig Claiborne includes a recipe for a 'Chrysanthemum Hot Pot' in *The Chinese Cookbook* (1972). Likely to have originated in Mongolia, as early as the tenth-century Liao Dynasty, and firmly established by the Mongolian Yuan Dynasty, hotpots were consumed in the winter months in China. Empress Dowager Cixi, because she was from the colder, northern region of China, is known to have enjoyed a chrysanthemum hotpot made in the imperial kitchen, which featured chrysanthemum blossoms floating in a vegetable and meat soup. In Guangdong in southeast China, snake and chrysanthemum is a favourite dish in the winter months. The snakes are kept alive in cages at speciality restaurants until needed, and the small white variety of chrysanthemum blossoms are included in the soup. Zhongshan City in the province of Zhongshan, China, known as the 'Town of Chrysanthemum', holds an annual festival exhibition of the flower, and also hosts a special chrysanthemum banquet that includes chrysanthemum fish meatballs, chrysanthemum cakes, chrysanthemum-brewed wine, chrysanthemum dumplings and other chrysanthemum-based dishes.

'Mums', botanically *Chrysanthemum morifolium*, came to Japan in the eighth century and became the flower representing the Japanese imperial family, symbolizing purity and perfection. Yellow, white and purple 'mums' are grown specifically as edible flowers: the blossoms are boiled to make a sweet drink, while in salads the raw flowers are a pungent, if not bitter, ingredient. Short, small petal varieties are often used to decorate sashimi dishes, while long petal varieties are used in small dishes such as *ohitashi*, *gomaae* (blanched and dressed with sesame dressing), *sunomono* (blanched and dressed with sweetened vinegar) and *tempura*. The flowers are also added to a *dashi*-based sauce thickened with potato starch or *kuzu*.

China's Chong Yang festival was later brought to Japan as *kiku-no-kisewata*. Sweet bean paste cakes, tinted pink and shaped like chrysanthemums, are a special treat served during this celebration. They are topped with a small dab of white bean paste that represents a little piece of cotton that would be placed on top of chrysanthemums on the festival's eve. The cotton is left overnight to absorb the dew. In the twelfth century people prayed for long life by purifying themselves with the dew-soaked cotton.

Both of these ceremonies are based on a mythical story about the magical powers of chrysanthemums and the *Kannon Sutra*, a popular devotional chant in Japanese Buddhism. According to the legend of Kikujido, if four lines of the sutra

Chrysanthemum wine is traditionally drunk during China's Double Ninth Festival. Sketch from anonymous 18th-century Chinese painting.

(four lines out of eight that praise the Kannon) are written on a chrysanthemum leaf, the dew that forms on this leaf will become an elixir that gives to those who drink it 800, 900 or even 1,000 years of life, along with a youthful appearance.

Daylily

Daylilies are not true lilies, an important distinction since many of their lily cousins are poisonous. Daylilies are mentioned in early written Chinese records as a food source. When the flowers are dried, they are referred to as 'golden needles'.

Golden needles are a traditional ingredient in Chinese hot and sour soup and *moo shu* pork. They can also be combined with a flour-based batter and made into fritters. The buds, which have a more vegetal taste akin to sweet, crisp lettuce, can be stir-fried.

'Buddha's delight' is a well-known vegetarian dish in Chinese and Buddhist cuisine. It was traditionally enjoyed by

Moo shu pork with dried daylilies ('golden needles').

Buddhist monks who are vegetarians, but has grown in popularity throughout the world as a common vegetarian dish available in Chinese restaurants. The dish consists of vegetables and other vegetarian ingredients, sometimes with the addition of seafood or eggs, which are cooked in soy-sauce-based liquid with other seasonings until tender. The specific ingredients vary greatly, but the dish is usually made with at least ten ingredients, including golden needles, which are generally available in dried form, although more elaborate versions may comprise eighteen or even 35 ingredients. The dish is traditionally served in Chinese households on the first day of the Chinese New Year, stemming from the old Buddhist practice that one should maintain a vegetarian diet in the first five days of the new year as a form of self-purification.

In addition to the lily-flower buds, lily bulbs are widely cultivated for food in Asia, especially in China, Korea and Japan. In China they are grown in both the northern and central regions. Although there are many species of lily with edible bulbs, the varieties most commonly grown for food in China are *Lilium brownii*, *L. dauricum* and *L. pumilum*. Bulbs from *L. brownii*, which have beautiful white trumpet-shaped flowers, are the ones usually available in the markets. For years only the dried bulb sections were available from China, but now fresh lily bulbs, which are in season from spring through late summer, can be obtained. They are sold vacuum-sealed in plastic and can be kept fresh for a few weeks in the refrigerator if left unopened.

In Japan, *yurine*, a type of cream-white daylily bulb that resembles garlic, is especially prized. The small segments are not usually served alone but are separated and steamed or boiled along with other ingredients. The flavour is mild and slightly sweet, and the texture is creamy.

Lotus

The lotus has long been a symbol for Buddhism throughout Asia, representing one's spiritual path towards the light of wisdom, clarity and compassion, finally blooming into perfection and enlightenment. The root of this beautiful flower is eaten during the New Year's celebrations as a reminder of this Buddhist ideal. In Hinduism, the lotus represents the gods Vishnu, Brahma and the goddesses Lakshmi and Saraswati. Representative of divine beauty and purity, Vishnu is often described as the 'Lotus-eyed One'. The creator god Brahma is believed to have emerged from the navel of Vishnu upon a lotus flower; the flower's unfolding petals suggest the expansion of the soul. Lotus flowers are placed on the altars as offerings, but the flower is also regularly eaten in many forms by the worshippers. The whole blossom, with stamens and sepals removed, is often battered and fried and then sprinkled with sugar. The stamen of the flower can be dried to make herbal tea.

All parts of this aquatic plant, from the roots to the seeds, are used in Chinese cooking. Empress Cixi, as previously mentioned, was said to have enjoyed lotus-flower-petal fritters. The seeds are enjoyed boiled, roasted and, if very young, eaten raw. Lotus is a staple at many banquets, where traditionally the holes in its sausage-shaped rhizome are often stuffed with meats or preserved fruits. Many foods at banquets and at ordinary meals are coated with lotus flour, then fried or steamed. Lotus flowers are also a traditional and beautiful garnish.

The sweet five-fruit soup, which contains lotus seeds, is a folk health food in Zhaozhou, China, where longan, gingko, lotus seeds, pearl barley and lily root are considered spleen-invigorating and health-improving foods. Five-fruit soup is

Lotus blossom.

The lotus has sacred symbolism in both Buddhism and Hinduism. Buddha is here sitting on a lotus.

eaten during the Chinese Spring Festival, beginning on the first day of the Chinese lunar New Year. The soup is cooked with pearl barley, gordon euryale seed, longan, lotus seed and beans, along with white sugar. Delicious and nourishing, it is served to guests from the first to the fifteenth day of the first lunar month. In Hangzhou, the lotus is made into a special sweet called lotus jelly, which, when made from the fresh plant, is popular around the New Year, symbolizing hope for a sweet year.

Lotus seed paste is a traditional filling for mooncakes, which are made for the popular mid-autumn festival throughout China. The sweet may also contain one or more whole salted egg yolks in the centre to symbolize the full moon. The mid-autumn festival is linked to the legends of Chang'e, the mythical Moon Goddess of Immortality. According to *Li-ji*, an ancient Chinese book recording customs and ceremonies, the Chinese emperor should offer sacrifices to the sun in spring and the moon in autumn: the fifteenth day of the eighth lunar month is called mid-autumn. The cakes have become so popular today that the festival itself is often called the Mooncake Festival. The traditional carved wooden moulds for mooncakes come in a myriad of shapes, including floral designs, and new flavours have been introduced, including rose-flavoured mooncakes.

Making its way to Japan from China, *renkon* (lotus root) can be found at Japanese markets. It has a strange tubular shape and brown skin that is sometimes speckled and somewhat dirty-looking. Peeling or scrubbing the skin reveals a pure, almost white interior and when sliced, its beautiful pattern of holes is revealed. The texture is hard and crunchy, so *renkon* is usually boiled in seasoned *dashi* or cut into paper-thin slices for a salad.

Lotus root served with broccoli. Both the lotus root (rhizome) and stem have a unique pattern of holes.

Banana Blossom

The equatorial climate regions of India permit a variety of fruits, vegetables and grains to be grown throughout the year, including many edible flowers. Over time, with the advent of Buddhism and Jainism, segments of the population began to embrace vegetarianism. Later, the Mughal, British and Portuguese influences added to the already diverse Indian cuisine. In accordance with Indian yogic traditions, a food classification system that categorized any food item as *saatvic*, *raajsic* or *taamsic* developed.

Many wild banana species, as well as cultivars, exist in extraordinary diversity in India, China and Southeast Asia.

Banana flowers (blossoms) in a street market in Hue, Vietnam.

There are fuzzy bananas whose skins are bubblegum pink; green-and-white striped bananas with pulp the colour of orange sherbet; and bananas that, when cooked, taste like strawberries. The name of the aromatic *go san heong* banana means, 'You can smell it from the next mountain.'

Culinary uses for the banana blossom or flower are just as varied, especially in Southeast Asia. Like the banana fruit itself, the banana flower also has a phallic shape, and both are regarded as signs of fertility. Bananas are rich in potassium and vitamin B, which are said to be necessary for sex-hormone production. A fresh, tender banana flower can be sliced and served raw. In Thailand, it is often accompanied by a hot and spicy dip called *nam prik*. South Indians make a recipe in which the chopped banana flower is steamed with salt, tempered with mustard seeds, *urad dal*, curry leaves and asafoetida and topped with grated coconut. Other Asian and Indian cuisines add the sliced banana flower to meat stews, stir-fries, soups, and rice or noodle combinations. It is also used in cold salads, with the salad mixture presented in one of the large purple-red outer leaves.

In the Philippines, *sabunganay*, as the banana blossom is known, is a preferred vegetable for *sinigang* (sour soup). Banana blossom may also be made into *adobo* with lots of onions and some garlic, some cracked pepper and vinegar to taste. It may be boiled and made as a salad with 'KBL' (*kamatis, bugguong,*

Banana flower salad.

lasona) and it can also be roasted and prepared as a salad, as 'meatballs' or even as an omelette.

In India, *mochar chop*, or *mochar ghonto*, is a banana blossom appetizer with coconut and peanuts, and a favourite street-food snack. *Mocha* is the Bengali name for banana blossoms. The banana plant is not only cultivated and consumed widely throughout Bengali culture, but its auspicious presence has special significance in religious rites, wedding rituals and festive traditions. Every part of the banana plant is used: the fruit, both ripe and unripe, cooked and uncooked; the flower (*mocha*) and the pith of the stem (*thor*); and the green banana peel, which can be cooked and eaten. Bengali chefs cook food wrapped in banana leaves to impart a special flavour and the large flat leaves of the banana plant are used as disposable plates.

Made with finely chopped banana blossom, *larb* is a type of salad based on minced meat that is often called the national dish of Laos, where the dish most likely originated. It is also popular in northeast Thailand. The meat in *larb* may be raw or cooked, and sometimes fish such as catfish are used instead of meat. Mint and other herbs feature strongly in the dish, and it is seasoned with lime juice, fish sauce and minced chilli peppers. Finely ground toasted rice is also an essential ingredient. Many variations of banana blossom salad can be found throughout Southeast Asia.

Indian sweet dishes are often seasoned with saffron and rose-petal essences as well as cardamom and nutmeg. A special symbolic meal of 56 courses, *Chappan Bhog*, is offered to Lord Krishna. This includes a number of dishes that contain floral colourings and flavourings, such as *boondi laddu*, *rasgoola*, *raj bhoga*, *sandesh*, *gulab jamun* and *jalebi*.

Other Asian Edible Flowers

There are many other edible flowers in use throughout Asia. The blue pea flower (*Clitoria ternatea*) is found in Singapore and Malaysia and has the appearance of human female genitalia, hence its name. The natural colouring extracted from the blue pea flower is used to create the beautiful blue *nonya kueh* (a glutinous sweet offered at weddings) called *pulit tai tai*. Torch ginger flowers (*Etlingera elatior*) are found in Indonesia, Thailand and other parts of Asia. They are used in making traditional *rojak*, a unique salad of fruit and shrimp paste. The flower buds are also used in *laksa*, a popular spicy noodle soup in Peranakan cuisine.

The Mavesi and Gaund people living in seven settlements in the Indian state of Uttar Pradesh have a diet largely consisting of mahua flowers (*Madhuca longifolia*). The flowers are dried in the sun and then eaten whole or mixed with rice or wheat gruel. The flowers are also used to make a syrup and fermented with granular molasses to make an alcoholic drink for celebrations. In India the white flowers of the neem tree (*Azadirachta indica*) are collected by spreading a clean cloth beneath the flowering tree. The flowers are dried and are used in a variety of ways, such as in neem flower rice, lentil spice mixes and *vepampoo rasam*, in which the bitter flowers symbolize the 'bitter' side of life that must be accepted along with the 'sweet' side.

The chopstick flower can be found in Vietnam's higher elevations. It grows in bunches of two colours, white and violet. Chopstick trees are tall and slim with lumpy bark and the fruits are long and thin like chopsticks. Together with linh fish, which is available in the same season, chopstick flowers create a popular sour soup. Each year during the flood season in southern Vietnam, people in the Mekong delta pick *dien*

dien flowers from the fields or canals to cook soup or to use in salads. Renting a boat to pick the flowers has become an attraction for visiting tourists.

The peony (*Paeonia lactiflora*) flower has long been an edible favourite in China, where the fallen petals are parboiled and sweetened as a teatime delicacy. Peony water was used for drinking in the Middle Ages. The petals can be added to a summer salad or floated in punches and lemonades.

For centuries, the Japanese have expressed their love for cherry blossoms (*Prunus serrulata*) in songs, poetry, horticulture and art. It should be no surprise then to find that cherry blossoms are also found in Japanese cuisine. The blossoms and leaves are pickled in *umeboshi* vinegar, the leaves sold in flat packages, the blossoms in jars. The blossoms may be eaten from the jar, although they are salty – rinsing them in water may be a good idea. A blossom or two added to a cup of tea creates a salty and sour sakura tea.

While Asian chefs have exhibited remarkable virtuosity in cooking with edible flowers, they have also elevated to a high degree the art of creating edible floral garnishes from a multitude of fruits and vegetables. The exquisite craft of fruit and vegetable carving developed very slowly in Asia, constantly adapting to the prosperity of the population. At the time of the Tang Dynasty (618–906) and the Sung Dynasty (960–1279) the garnishing of food was already widespread in China, even among the middle classes. In Japan, the Kaiseki meal, accompanying a traditional tea ceremony, will often contain elegant edible flower garnishes.

5

The Mediterranean and the Middle East

Over the ages, a variety of edible flowers have made their way into the cuisines of people living in the Mediterranean region. Poppy, carnation, lotus, nasturtium, fennel blossom, cloves, roses and calendula were just a few of the flowers cultivated and eaten by Mediterranean civilizations. Four edible flowers of the region that have achieved a global following are saffron, artichoke, capers and orange blossom.

Saffron

Saffron was at least partly responsible for the rich exchange of art and architecture, science and technology, and even philosophy between Europe, the Middle East and Asia, as the golden dried stigmas of the flower travelled across ancient trade routes or were brought back to Europe by conquering crusaders. Quite an accomplishment for such a little flower.

The autumn-flowering crocus, *Crocus sativus*, has been valued since ancient times for its scent and flavouring properties, as well as for its role as a colouring agent, creating a rich golden colour. Each flower contains just three stigmas and these can only be harvested by hand, making the growing and harvesting of saffron a laborious and costly endeavour.

It is little wonder that only the rich and powerful could afford the spice. Even today a pound (450 g) of pure saffron may retail at $3,000 or more, as it is made up of 225,000 hand-picked, dried stigmas from 75,000 flowers. At such exorbitant prices, it is unlikely you would follow the ancient Roman practice of stuffing your pillowcase with saffron to ease a hangover. Nor would you sleep on a bed of saffron as did the Roman god Zeus. True saffron aficionados, however, are prepared to pay such high prices for pure saffron rather than accept the cheaper adulterated form, which is usually mixed with safflower, a completely different flower with yellow dye properties. Although it is a common practice and legal today, such adulteration of saffron in the court of Henry VIII of England would have cost the perpetrator his head. Fourteenth-century German dealers who adulterated the spice could also expect the death sentence, in their case being burned at the stake.

The origin of saffron is still unclear, with some scholars citing India and others attributing Asia Minor as its source. But as far back as 40,000 to 50,000 years ago people living in the Fertile Crescent between the Tigris and Euphrates rivers used saffron as a pigment in cave paintings. The flower was well-known to the Sumerians both as a bright yellow dye and for its medicinal properties. Phoenician traders are credited with disseminating the flower through the Mediterranean region. One of the earliest references to saffron being used as a culinary item is found in the Hebrew Song of Solomon, dating from about 2,000 BCE, in which the flower was revered as a sweet-smelling spice.

After the fall of Rome, saffron production throughout the Mediterranean region sharply declined. However, with the intercultural exchanges brought about by trade on the Silk Road and also the expeditions of the Crusaders, the golden dried stigmas of the crocus flower once again attained a lofty status among the rich and powerful.

Between 1347 and 1350 the Black Death threatened the lives of millions of people, and the demand for saffron as a supposedly effective medicine against the disease skyrocketed. With most of the prime saffron-growing areas located in Muslim lands, and cut off to European traders by the Crusades, what saffron could be found had to be imported through places such as Rhodes. A fourteen-week 'saffron war' in 1374 erupted between European noblemen and the rising merchant class when a group of noblemen hijacked an 800-lb (360-kg) shipment of saffron valued at $500,000 in today's U.S. dollars. Although the saffron was recovered, saffron piracy remained a lucrative business until cultivation centres in Europe finally evolved.

Today, the world's supply of saffron comes primarily from Spain (specifically in the Castilla–La Mancha region), Egypt, Greece, Kashmir, Morocco and Iran, with the latter accounting for around 90–93 per cent of recent annual world production. No matter where the spice originates, it has become an essential part of the culinary culture of countries all around the globe. This is especially true of the Mediterranean region, where saffron is an important ingredient in French *bouillabaisse* and Italian *risotto Milanese* and where no reputable Spanish chef would dream of making *paella* or *arroz con pollo* without the best saffron. Saffron connoisseurs describe its aroma as reminiscent of metallic honey, while its taste has been described as hay-like and sweet. It also contributes a luminous yellow-orange colouring to foods.

From the Mediterranean region, saffron spread throughout Europe. In the seventeenth century the town of Saffron Walden in England was a major producer of saffron and the flower was so important to the local economy that it is depicted on the town's coat of arms. Eighteenth-century German settlers in Pennsylvania – misleadingly called the 'Pennsylvania Dutch' – brought saffron with them from Germany and soon established a thriving business in cultivating and exporting the spice, an enterprise that flourished until the War of 1812 brought it to a halt. The German saffron-farmers treasured the flower and made beautiful wooden boxes, which resembled goblets with lids, in which to store saffron. They were decorated with painted garlands and wreaths. The boxes

Saffron is a unique ingredient in Persian saffron ice cream.

The coat of arms of Saffron Walden, England, once a major saffron cultivation centre.

today are considered pieces of folk art, with the works of the nineteenth-century farmer-craftsman Joseph Lehn often selling for $48,000 or more at auction.

Artichoke

Another popular edible flower of the Mediterranean region that has gained favour throughout the world is the artichoke. Although its leathery leaves and large size – the artichoke plant is about 6 feet (2 metres) in diameter and sometimes over 6 feet tall – give it an otherworldly appearance, ancient peoples of the Mediterranean region found the unopened flower bud a delicious addition to their cuisine. The many edible, leaf-like parts that make up the bud are called scales. The base of the bud, the heart, is also edible. Known botanically as *Cynara scolymus*, the artichoke is technically a thistle. Although there are as many as fifty types of artichokes worldwide, the Green Globe or Italian variety is the most commonly used in the kitchen. If allowed to flower, the artichoke bud opens up to a lovely violet-blue flower measuring almost 7 in. (18 cm) in diameter.

Over 2,000 years ago people found edible the three wild species of artichoke that grew in the central and western

Artichokes displayed in a Vietnamese market.

Henrietta Shore, *Artichoke Pickers*, 1934.

Mediterranean basin and Canary Islands, the Aegean Islands and southern Turkey, Syria, Lebanon and Israel. These plants were known as cardoons and still exist in the wild in various locations throughout the region. Although the artichokes of today were probably cultivated from the wild plants of Sicily or Tunisia, the name comes from the Arabic *al'qarshuf*, given to the plant by Moroccan invaders to Spain who introduced artichokes to that area. In Spain, the name became *alcachofa* and in Italy *carciofa*.

As early as 300 BCE the Greek philosopher and naturalist Theophrastus wrote of artichokes being grown in Italy and Sicily. The ancient Greek physician Dioscorides praised the artichoke for its medicinal benefits and the flower was highly prized by rich Greeks and Romans – although Pliny the Elder called artichoke 'one of the earth's monstrosities'. It was preserved in honey and vinegar seasoned with laserwort and cumin. As with saffron, the fall of Rome resulted in the loss of artichoke cultivation, except for small pockets, most likely in monasteries, where the plant continued to be cultivated. In the fifteenth century artichokes once again whetted the taste buds of the ruling elite when in 1466 a member of the influential Strozzi family brought some from Florence to Naples, where they became an instant hit. In 1576 Bartolomeo Boldo wrote about the artichoke: 'It has the virtue of provoking Venus for both men and women; for women making them more desirable and helping men who are in these matters rather tardy.'

Due to the rather tedious manner in which artichokes must be eaten, Italian cooks serve them primarily as starters or as a separate course during the meal. They may be served with dipping sauces such as hollandaise, vinegar, melted butter, aioli, lemon juice or a mayonnaise and Parmesan cheese dip, but they are also routinely stuffed with meat, fish, poultry or fresh vegetables and served in a variety of ways: raw, boiled, steamed, fried or marinated. Artichokes may also be made into herbal teas or into an Italian liqueur called Cynar.

The Mediterranean region still produces most of the world's supply of artichokes, with Italy, Spain and France leading the way. Within the United States, California provides 100 per cent of the crop, with 80 per cent of that coming from Monterey County. Artichokes grew in Thomas Jefferson's garden and had been introduced into Louisiana by the French; as early as 1806, instructions for planting artichokes appeared in gardening books. In the 1890s Sicilian immigrants began cultivating them in California and by 1904 were shipping them to the east coast. It wasn't long before the Mafia took control of most of the produce. In the 1920s gangsters terrorized artichoke distributors and growers alike, going so far as to send henchmen armed with machetes into the fields in the dead of night to hack down artichoke plants. In his own war with the mafia, the 'artichoke wars' caused Mayor Fiorello La Guardia of New York to declare the 'sale, display and possession' of artichokes illegal in 1935, a ban he could keep in effect for only one week.

Artichokes have always been planted, cultivated and harvested by hand. The peak harvest season is between late March and May, with a smaller harvest in the autumn. Fields may be picked thirty times a year. All of this meticulous handwork yields a premium-quality crop, but at the same time it is the reason why artichokes are not commonly seen on everyday menus.

Capers

The writer and film-maker Nora Ephron wrote in *Heartburn* (1983): 'Some people *pretend* to like capers, but the truth is that any dish that tastes good with capers in it tastes even better with capers not in it.' Despite Ephron's acerbic wit, there are many people who enjoy the sharp, piquant flavour of capers, indulging in a culinary tradition that is thousands of years old.

Caper plants (*Capparis spinosa*) are native to the Mediterranean area, especially in Cyprus, Egypt, France, Greece, Israel, Italy, Morocco, Spain and Turkey. Caper bushes are hardy and flourish in dry heat and intense sunlight, and they thrive in poor, unfertilized soil. Up to 3 feet (1 metre) in diameter, the plants rarely grow taller than 2 feet. Some caper bushes are cultivated but most grow wild. An opportunistic plant, caper bushes can be found growing in cracks in rocks, pavement and walls, and can even be seen clinging to the famous Wailing Wall in Jerusalem. Although the plant can produce delicate and fragrant white flowers, these are rarely seen because it is the unopened flower bud that is harvested and then pickled in salt, brine or vinegar for consumption.

Capers add pungency, saltiness and a unique aroma to many foods, such as pasta sauces, pizza, fish, meats and salads, and they are an important part of Mediterranean cuisine, along with olives, rocket (arugula), artichokes and anchovies. The flavour of capers, often referred to as similar to mustard and black pepper, is due to the mustard oil, methyl

Illustration of a caper plant by Otto Wilhelm Thomé (1840–1925).

Caper plants blooming from the Wailing Wall in Jerusalem.

isothiocyanate, produced in crushed plant tissues. They are an essential ingredient in signature Cypriot, Italian, Maltese and Sicilian dishes such as chicken or veal piccata, spaghetti puttanesca, caponata and Niçoise salad.

As far back as 2000 BCE, the Sumerians used capers medicinally in a wide variety of applications, especially as a digestive aid. The ancient Greeks learned the secret of transforming the unopened flower buds into a gastronomic treat and benefitted economically from a robust trading of capers throughout the Mediterranean region. The Hebrews regarded the caper as an aphrodisiac. The New Living Translation of Ecclesiastes 12:5 warns:

> Remember him before you become fearful of falling and worry about danger in the streets; before your hair turns white like an almond tree in bloom, and you drag

along without energy like a dying grasshopper, and the caperberry no longer inspires sexual desire.

Harvesting capers is hard work. Pickers must squat on their haunches to reach the low bushes, working from the tips of the branches where the smallest, most desirable buds are located, down towards the base of the plant, where the larger buds can be found. The pickers work quickly and deftly without gloves, careful to avoid the sharp thorns located behind each bud. They must also be careful not to snap any branches, since that would prohibit capers from growing the following year.

Today, the largest producer of capers is Morocco, followed by Spain and Turkey. Italy, once the king of caper cultivation, now produces only small amounts, primarily on the island of Pantelleria in Sicily. Pantelleria capers are the only IGP (Indicazione Geografica Protetta) certified capers. La Nicchia farm on Pantelleria began picking capers in 1949 and the activity continues according to the local tradition and culture. The farm continually develops new caper products; one of them, crunchy capers, is said to taste like bacon bits and could be the next new pizza topping. La Nicchia also makes a caper powder used in molecular gastronomy.

Orange Blossom

It is not clear when orange trees (*Citrus sinensis*), originating in southern China and northeastern India, first appeared in the Mediterranean area, but by the eighth century the Arab world had already discovered how to steam-distil the fragrant white blossoms of the orange tree to produce orange-flower water and its essential oil, neroli, which was used as a fragrance and perfume. It is a relatively expensive oil since it takes one ton of orange blossoms to produce a litre of oil. Islamic cuisine employed it in spicy meat dishes of goat and lamb, a wide variety of wheat products such as flatbreads and sweetened baked goods, and confections. Typically, these foods would be aromatized and flavoured with edible flowers or flower water. Rose- and orange-flower waters were favourites. With the rise of Islam in the centuries following the death of Mohammed in 632, Perso–Islamic cuisine, as it is called, spread throughout the Mediterranean area, including North Africa, Spain and southern France.

By the eighth century the most extensive collection of cookbooks up to that time could be found in Baghdad, the most famous being the *Baghdad Cookbook*, which contained over 300 recipes, twenty of them contributed by the caliph Harun al-Rashid. Some of the recipes are for sweet drinks flavoured and perfumed with rose- or orange-blossom water and these same waters were also combined with various spices to create tantalizing new taste sensations.

By the sixteenth century orange-blossom water was being used in Sicily as a flavouring agent, especially in sweets. The orange tree was fairly widespread throughout Europe by the seventeenth century, particularly the bitter orange, also known as sour orange, marmalade orange or Seville orange, named after the Spanish city that boasts as many as 14,000 orange trees lining its streets. To make orange-blossom water, the flowers are hand-picked when they are fully expanded. The blossoms are then placed in a net sack and distilled in water in a copper pot. It takes approximately 2 lb (900 g) of blossoms to produce a single quart of distillate.

Orange-blossom water is a key ingredient in the French *gibassier* (a pastry from Provence), *pompe à l'huile* (a Provencal Christmas pastry) and madeleines, in the Spanish *roscon de reyes* (king cake), and in the Italian *panna cotta* and *pastiera*, an Easter pie. Orange-blossom water has long been a traditional ingredient in a variety of North African and Middle Eastern dishes, especially sweets and baked goods. Orange-blossom water mixed with honey is used in Arab variants of baklava. In Morocco, orange-blossom water is still used as a perfume when guests are invited to wash their hands as they enter a house or before drinking tea. While this traditional use for orange-blossom water is dying out, it is still widely used in cooking as an ingredient in the crescent-shaped *ka'b el ghzal* (gazelle's horns) and the snake-like *m'hanncha* (the snake) pastries, as well as other desserts.

One explanation for the popularity of orange-blossom water in Mediterranean cuisine might be its long association with fertility and good fortune. The Greek goddess Hera received orange blossoms as a symbol of purity and virginity when she married Zeus, as did the Roman goddess

Turkish pastries often feature orange-blossom water as an essential ingredient.

Jean-Baptiste-Simeon Chardin, *La Brioche*, 1763, garnished with orange blossom as a symbol of marriage.

Juno when she married Jupiter. Over the centuries, orange blossoms have been incorporated into bridal bouquets and head wreaths. Queen Victoria wore a wreath of orange blossoms in her wedding to Prince Albert, forsaking all of her innumerable jewelled tiaras. However, orange blossoms may also signify seduction, as prostitutes in Madrid used to wear a few drops of neroli oil as a means of luring clients.

Orange-blossom water may be added to tea, mineral water and other drinks (in nineteenth-century America, John Pemberton included neroli oil in one of the early recipes for his new soft drink, Coca-Cola) and to custards, puddings, ice cream and candies. The fragrant and unique orange-blossom honey is a delicacy created as the flowers are in bloom. In the Mediterranean region, France, Israel, Italy and Spain are

Orange-blossom honey and orange-flower water are widely available in food shops.

the major producers of orange-blossom honey but it has found favour in other countries as well. In the United States, producers in Florida, New York and Texas supply much of the demand for the honey, although the honey is made from sweeter varieties of orange than the bitter orange.

Other Edible Flowers of the Mediterranean and Middle East Region

There are many other edible flowers found in the cuisine of the Mediterranean and Middle East. Anchusa (*Anchusa azurea*), also known as Italian bugloss, is noted for its brilliant sapphire-blue flowers and is related to borage. The flower pairs well with fish, salads and desserts and may also be crystallized. Tunisians make a soup of anchusa and sorrel.

Originating in ancient Greece, dandelions were one of the 'bitter herbs' mentioned in the Old Testament. The buds and leaves may be cooked and served like spinach and they also make an excellent salad. Italians are fond of dandelions and may have been the inventors of dandelion wine, made from the petals of the flower.

The flowers of the mint plant (*Mentha*) have the same taste as the leaves, but are milder. Several varieties can be used in custards, desserts or with vegetables and curries. It is often found in Middle East dishes such as tabbouleh or couscous.

Also known as bellflower – among other names – the edible flowers of campanula (*Campanula rapunculoides*) range in colour from white to pink, blue, mauve and a variegated variety called pantaloon. Mainly used in salads, bellflower can also be used in confits and jellies. Crystallized, the showy flowers make beautiful dessert decorations.

Hyssop (*Agastache foeniculum*), also known as anise, is native to the Eastern Mediterranean area and Asia. Its small blue-violet flowers have been used since biblical times. The flowers have a liquorice-aniseed taste and fragrance and can be made into a sauce served with lamb or used as a flavouring in biscuits (cookies). The Chinese traditionally add it to some stir-fried beef dishes. Mustard greens (*Brassica juncea* or *Brassica nigra*) are commonly used in salads, but ancient Romans used mustard flowers for their supposed aphrodisiacal qualities. Ancient apothecaries pounded the flowers into a powder using a mortar and pestle and sold them as love potions.

The unopened flowers of the cassia (cinnamon) tree are picked just before blooming and dried in the sun. Commonly used for pickling and mulling spice blends, the cassia buds look like small cloves with a flavour similar to cinnamon but with more of a floral, wine scent. The large okra (*Abelmoschus esculentus*) flower blooms for only one day, so chefs need to be quick if they intend to use the flower in their dishes. The ancient Egyptians cultivated okra and ate its pale yellow flower petals, which resemble hibiscus. Both okra and its flower are still used today in Egyptian stews.

6

Europe

Flowers are appreciated worldwide for their colours, fragrances and, in the case of edible flowers, their distinctive flavours. They have also, for many cultures, become iconographic – living symbols of virtues and emotions. In Europe, especially in Victorian England, an entire floriography, a 'language of flowers', developed in which feelings and emotions could be exchanged between people simply based upon the flowers they chose to give and receive.

Victorians were particularly flower-crazy. Flower arrangements could be found everywhere in a Victorian home, and flower patterns were common in fine china, stationery, wall coverings, carpets and more. Fashionable women might have worn flowers in their hair, pinned to their clothing or as jewellery, while men would wear boutonnières, floral suit decorations. Candied flowers were placed on top of cakes. Flower bouquets were given on a variety of occasions and often exchanged specifically to convey a message to someone. 'Tussie-mussies' were small flower bouquets wrapped in a lace doily and tied with a satin ribbon. The exact choice of flowers in the bouquet, the colours, even how the flowers were arranged – an upright flower represented a positive thought while one pointing downwards indicated a negative thought – were all carefully considered by the sender so that his or her message would not be misconstrued. If that message seemed unclear to the recipient, one could always consult one of the many flower dictionaries that were in vogue at the time in order to better decipher it.

Hundreds of flowers were assigned meanings in floriographies of the day. A yellow carnation signified disappointment or rejection, hibiscus meant consumed by love, elderflower symbolized zeal, lavender stood for love and violet indicated modesty or virtue.

Rose

The rose is an excellent example of how flowers can be used as a means of communication. Generally, roses symbolize love, passion, desire and sex; lovers have traditionally exchanged roses, and more than one romance novel has featured a bed strewn with rose petals. Since they symbolize love and passion, the addition of rose petals to any dish makes it romantic and sexy. Quail served with a rose-petal sauce was the memorably sensuous dish in Laura Esquivel's novel *Like Water for Chocolate* (1989).

In addition to the amorous and emotional impact of the rose, it has also been used for centuries to create culinary delights in the kitchen, where it is valued for its flavour and versatility. The well-known flowering shrubs of the genus *Rosa* can be traced back to the ancient civilizations of Persia, Egypt, Babylon and China. One of the earliest recordings of its culinary usage dates back to ancient Mesopotamia, around the seventh century BCE. Here, in the cuneiform tablets of the era, roses are described as an essential ingredient in medicinal preparations. Roses were probably first cultivated in ancient Persia, where there is evidence that rose wine was made and exported as far back as 2,000 years ago.

The petals of most species can be eaten or used to flavour foods, either directly or in the form of rosewater, which is obtained by the distillation of petals. For Greeks, the rose was symbolic of love, beauty and happiness. The Latin word *rosa* comes from the Greek word for red, *rodos*. Roses, which were used as a seasoning, were sold by the roadside in fourth-century BCE Athens. In ancient Greece, rose fragrance was considered appropriate for a drinking party, and in both Greece and Rome rose essence was also sometimes used to season wine. The Romans, who associated the rose with Venus, the goddess of love, also scented their wine with rose petals.

By the tenth century rose water had become a commonly used flavour for cakes, cookies and pastries. During the medieval period, rose flavouring was used extensively in poultry, game and fish recipes. Royal chefs prepared many main courses with roses and added the flavouring to desserts such as pastries and candies. Rose preserves also enjoyed popularity during that time. The use of rosewater spread to Europe via the Crusades from regions such as present-day Persia, where it had been distilled on a large scale from as early as the ninth century. Marzipan, which originated in the Middle East and arrived in Western Europe by the Middle Ages, had long been flavoured with rosewater.

Rosewater became increasingly popular in European cuisine during the Renaissance. In *Da Vinci's Kitchen: A Secret History of Italian Cuisine* (2006), author Dave Dewitt cites two Renaissance recipes that use rosewater. The first, for 'the best Bisket-Cakes', reads:

> Take four new laid Eggs, leave out two of the Whites, beat them very well, then put in two spoonfuls of

Any culinary product that contains roses, such as the products pictured here, is considered sexy and romantic.

Rose-water, and beat them very well together, then put in a pound of double refin'd Sugar beaten and searced [sifted], and beat them together one hour, then cut to them one pound of fine Flower, and still beat them together a good while; then put them upon Plates rubbed over with Butter, and set them unto the Oven as fast as you can, have care you do not bake them too much.

The second recipe, for Shrewsbury cakes, requires 'a little rosewater' for flavouring. *Tourte aux pommes et aux poires*, a classic Renaissance dessert, is most likely the ancestor of our contemporary apple pie and also contains rosewater. John Murrell's *Two Books of Cookerie and Carving* (1638) describes a recipe for pickled rosebuds: 'Pick rosebuds and put them in an earthen pipkin, with white wine vinegar and sugar and so you may use cowslips, violets, or rosemary flowers.'

The medieval town of Provins in northwest France is known for food products created from roses. The 'rosa gallica' was already praised by the Greek poet Anacreon in the sixth century BCE, and it was probably brought to Gaul (France) with the Roman conquest. The cultivation of *Rosa gallica officinalis* declined in Provins during the eighteenth and nineteenth centuries, but today it has gained a comeback of sorts. The rose is still strongly associated with Provins' confectionery

French chef Pierre Hermé's cult favourite macaron, the Ispahan, is filled with delicate rose-flavoured cream.

creativity, including products such as candied rose petals, rose-flavoured honey, chocolate, liqueur and fruit jelly sweets.

In the Victorian era roses were used as a flavouring agent in tea, sweets, pastry, oil, conserves and sauces. Rose-flavoured honey became a popular preserve for ham, and rose-flavoured vinegar was used to dress greens and vegetable dishes. Rosewater was also used to make Waverly jumbles, an old British baked good that was served in the United States in President James Monroe's White House.

Rose gardens were an essential part of an elegant Victorian lifestyle. Stylish ladies met for afternoon teas in parlours that were decorated with freshly cut roses. Rose flavouring was an elegant addition to the food and beverages served at these affairs. The Victorians were especially fond of rose-petal sandwiches, which were made of dark-red roses on thin slices of bread with real country butter or famous English thick cream.

According to Linda Ziedrich, writing in *The Joy of Jams, Jellies and Other Sweet Preserves* (2009), roses fell out of favour when other flavourings began to become more fashionable:

> In Europe, the culinary use of roses declines with the introduction of vanilla and in the u.s. roses have never been a popular flavoring. Though Martha Washington's *Booke of Cookery* contained many recipes using rosewater – the recipes had been passed on to her from her English ancestors – very few flower recipes are to be found in American 19th-century cookbooks.

But the use of roses is now experiencing a global renaissance, especially in baking. Rose flavouring once again gently graces some of the finest pastries created in the world's most exquisite European bakeries. The famed French pastry chef

Pierre Hermé has been exploring the relationship between perfume and cuisine, and in the process creating actually edible perfume. Along with his friend Jean-Michel Duriez, a 'nose' at the perfumer Rochas, the duo are breaking new ground in culinary exploration. A cult favourite created by Hermé is the Ispahan, named after the beautiful rose varietal, which consists of two large macarons filled with delicate rose-flavoured cream surrounded by fresh tangy raspberries and sweet lychee.

Violet

According to Victorian floriography, the violet (*Viola odorata*) symbolizes constancy, modesty, virtue, affection, watchful-ness, faithfulness, love and 'let's take a chance on happiness'. A familiar garden flower indigenous to Europe and North Africa but introduced throughout the world, violet petals are used as a fragrant flavouring. Throughout the years violets have also used been used for medicinal purposes, usually in the form of a tea. In Pakistan, the tea is drunk to increase sweating and thus reduce fever. It is also reputed to relieve anxiety and insomnia and to reduce high blood pressure. In the seventeenth century throat lozenges made with violet con-serve were used to treat bronchitis, as well as to combat sinus congestion. Violet sugar, used to treat consumption, was a popular staple in apothecaries of the time. These treatments using violets were quite effective because of the antibacterial properties of the blossoms.

Interestingly, violets contain salicylic acid, the chief ingredient in aspirin, and also high levels of vitamins A and C. In *Stalking the Healthful Herbs* (2005), Euell Gibbons writes about watching his Pennsylvania Dutch neighbours gather violets in the spring and include them with wild greens that they fed to their families: 'The Pennsylvania Dutch children are wise in eating violet blossoms, for these tasty little flowers are three times as rich in vitamin C, weight for weight, as oranges.'

Violets are frequently used in flavoured sugars. Anis de Flavigny are aniseed, sugar-coated candies formed into small, round white balls called *pastilles*. Originally made by Benedictine monks in Flavigny, France, they found favour among the French aristocracy; Madame de Pompadour was one famous fan. Today only one company, La Maison Troubat, makes these *pastilles*, using an ancient process called panning, in which the aniseeds and flavoured sugar syrup are tumbled together so that the sugar slowly builds up on the seed. The process takes fifteen days to complete. Violet is one of ten flavours of *pastilles* offered by the company.

Violet-flavoured sugar was a favourite of Edward I of England, along with rose sugar. His household documents dated from the year 1287 record that 300 lb (136 kg) of violet sugar were used. Charles II was very fond of violet sugar in the form of lozenges, or 'plates' as they were called. Violets are most often used in the kitchen in their candied form. In the Victorian times sugared violets were so popular that they were often served as a confection at high tea. They were also used to garnish cakes, pastries, flans and puddings. The Duchess of Kent, the mother of Queen Victoria, especially liked a violet tea made with a teaspoon of dried violets in a cup of boiling water, sweetened with honey. Queen Victoria commanded the royal gardener not to be without fresh violets for her tea, syrups, honey and jellies.

An interesting note about violets is that the perception of their taste and fragrance will differ among people. Violets contain a compound called ionone which interferes with our

Almost any edible flower can be made into a jam, jelly or confit.

olfactory receptors. After just a few whiffs of the flower it becomes impossible to detect its fragrance. There is also a genetic component to how we taste ionone. While some people may detect a soapy flavour, rather than a floral one, others may not taste or smell it at all.

Combining wine with violets dates back to the days of the ancient Greeks, who would not only put the petals in the wine, but scatter them all about their banquet halls. They also wore garlands decorated with violets in the belief that this would help to prevent dizziness and headaches from over-indulging in drink. John Gerard's sixteenth-century *Herbal* quotes Pliny speaking of violets, which he says 'are well used in garlands as smelt unto; and are good against heaviness of the head'.

Many cultures, including the Celts and the Germans, celebrate the arrival of springtime at the first sighting of violets. The Germans further celebrate this event with dancing and drinking of May wine, made of wine, herbs and, of course, violets. A traditional concoction from Austria is crème de violette, an infusion of violets, sugar and alcohol which has a rich, deep purple colour. Crème de violette has long been used in Austria by bakers who added it to chocolates and cakes, but it has come into vogue as a liqueur and cocktail ingredient. Another purple liqueur that may contain either violets or roses is Parfait Amour.

Violet sweets have been known for centuries. Howard's Violet were first made in New York City in the 1920s and are still sold today.

Culinary violets were known outside Europe as well. In 1886 the British immigrant to America William G. Stanford, who had settled in Rhinebeck, New York, recalled the profusion of violets at Easter in his native England and persuaded his brother George, a gardener, to join him in America and to bring with him a stock of double Parma violets. The brothers initiated a violet-growing industry in the small towns of the Hudson River Valley, which then caught on with the publication in 1902 of George Saltford's *How to Make Money Growing Violets*. In no time at all Rhinebeck became known as the 'Violet Capital of the World'.

In the 1920s Charles Howard sold small, square hard violet sweets which he named, aptly, Violet, on New York City street corners. By the 1930s the candy could be found in stores. Although violet cultivation in New York collapsed around the same time as a result of a killing fungus, the Great Depression and changing styles and tastes, Howard's violet candy survived and is still sold today.

Lavender

Traditionally, lavender has not been seen as a culinary herb, and its use in the kitchen is relatively recent. The name 'lavender' is derived from the Latin *lavare*, meaning to wash, and refers to the ancient use of this herb in baths to purify the body. Known in Greece as nard and in India as spikenard, oil of lavender found use across many cultures in cosmetics, massage oils and medicines. The Egyptians used unguents containing lavender to embalm their dead, and the Bible recounts two incidents in which Jesus is anointed with lavender oil (referred to as spikenard), symbolically foreshadowing his own death.

Elizabeth I, 16th-century painting. Elizabeth I of England was reported to have drunk ten cups of lavender tea a day for her headaches and insomnia.

Although long known for its healing, antiseptic and cleaning properties throughout the ages, the use of lavender fell into decline after the fall of the Roman Empire. Were it not for the monastery gardens of the Middle Ages where lavender was cultivated and used by monks and nuns, the herb's utility may have been lost to the modern age. Merton Abbey near London became the centre of lavender production in England. An important and expensive commodity, lavender sales helped raise money for the coffers of Edward I, according to the 1301 records of the Merton Priory.

When Henry VIII dissolved the Catholic monasteries in England in 1536, lavender found its way into the gardens of the aristocracy, where it was used to freshen the air and clothing. It was also used as an insect repellent and, in beeswax, as a furniture polish. Elizabeth I (1533–1603) brewed a lavender tea to ease her migraine headaches and was reported to have drunk up to ten cups a day. A lavender lover, Elizabeth demanded fresh lavender flowers in all her rooms daily and also insisted upon a conserve of lavender to be served with her meat at every meal. A recipe for lavender conserve from 1635 in *The Queen's Closet Opened* reads: 'Take the flowers being

THE
Queens
CLOSET
OPENED:
Incomparable SECRETS in
Physick, Chyrurgery, Preserving and Candying, &c.
Which were presented unto the
QUEEN
By the most Experienced Persons of the
Times, many whereof were had in
esteem, when she pleased to descend
to private Recreations.

Corrected and reviewed, with many Additions:
together with three exact Tables.

Vivit post funera Virtus.

LONDON,
Printed by J. G. for Nath. Brook, at the
Angel in Cornhill, 1663.

The Queen's Closet Opened (1658) contains numerous cake recipes using edible flowers.

new so many as you please, and beat them with three times their weight of White Sugar, after the same manner as Rosemary flowers; they will keep one year.'

In sixteenth-century France, lavender was believed to offer protection against the bubonic plague. A bit of lavender folklore from that period concerns a concoction of lavender, garlic, vinegar and other ingredients supposedly invented by thieves that allowed them to rob the houses of plague victims without contracting the disease themselves. Fittingly, the mixture was called Four Thieves Vinegar.

In the sixteenth and seventeenth centuries, lavender became extensively used in cooking, adding not only fragrance to food but a unique flavour as well, somewhat like rosemary but with a slight peppery kick. Of the several varieties of

Herbes de Provence is a traditional French spice mix usually containing lavender.

Lavender cupcakes.

lavender the most commonly used in cooking are varieties of English lavender (*Lavandula angustifolia*). The lower camphor and resin content of English lavender make it the preferred variety among many chefs. Used as a savoury herb, lavender was paired with various meats, especially lamb, for which it seems to have a particular affinity. In fact, in France lambs were grazed on lavender whenever possible. The small purple lavender flowers were often sprinkled over roasts to impart their flavour to the meat. For many years in Provence, lavender had been mixed with rosemary, savory, thyme and basil to create a spicy mixture for seasoning grilled meats, seafood, poultry and salads. In the 1970s this traditional mixture became commercially available as *herbes de Provence*. Although lavender was not one of the traditional ingredients always included in *herbes de Provence*, it has recently been added to several spice mixture brands to appeal to tourists who associate Provence with its many lavender fields.

Lavender has its sweet side, too. Mixing lavender flowers into sugar and sealing the mixture tightly for a couple of weeks results in a more exotic sugar that can be used in cakes, biscuits (cookies), buns and custards in place of regular sugar. Then there are candied lavender flowers, a product of the Victorian era's passion for all things floral. Queen Victoria was an avid user of lavender and went as far as to grant Sarah Sprule, a distiller of flowers, the title of 'Purveyor of Lavender Essence to the Queen' after a visit the queen and Princess Louise made to the distillery in 1886; Sarah's lavender water also earned her medals at exhibitions in Jamaica and Chicago.

Today, lavender is commonly used in rubs and seasonings for meat, fish, poultry and salads; as sugar and syrup for flavouring baked goods, ice cream and teas; and in butter, crème fraîche and preserved lavender lemons.

Elderflower

In Hans Christian Andersen's fairy tale 'The Elderflower Mother', a little boy's wild imaginings are attributed to a few cups of elderflower tea given to him by his mother. Although this quality of elderflower is an invention of the author, Andersen certainly was aware of the otherworldy reputation associated with not only elderflowers, but the entire elder tree (*Sambucus*).

One common belief held that witches could turn themselves into elder trees, and to cut one down or burn one was to court disaster at the hands of the hag. A line from the *Wiccan Rede*, written in England in the 1960s, says: 'Elder be ye Lady's tree, burn it not or cursed ye'll be.' This connection to black magic was prevalent throughout Europe. Elderflowers were a common ingredient in love potions, since an old tradition holds that they are aphrodisiacs. That tradition still exists. In Tempe, Arizona, Caffe Boa serves up a drink called Love Potion that incorporates elderflower liqueur while Ben Ford's Filling Station, located in Los Angeles International Airport of all places, serves a drink called Love Potion #10 that includes elderflower cordial or syrup.

The medicinal qualities of the elder tree have also been known since antiquity. Pliny wrote about the Roman usage of various parts of the tree as medicine. Ancient English and Welsh physicians knew the cooling effect of elderflower. In 1644 Dr Martin Blockwich authored a book titled *The Anatomie of the Elder* in which he meticulously described the medicinal qualities of the tree's flowers, leaves, berries, pith, bark and roots.

The small white or cream-coloured flowers of the black or blackberry elder (*Sambucus nigra*) are found in large clusters and bloom for only about three weeks in May through June, before producing black berries. The French, Austrians and Central Europeans make an elderflower syrup from the extract of elderflower blossoms.

Throughout much of Central, Eastern, and Southeastern Europe elderflower syrup is diluted with water to create a flavourful drink. Elderflower syrup is the basis for Fanta's Shokata soft drink, marketed in fifteen countries worldwide. St Germain, a French liqueur, is made from elderflowers and the Swedish akavit Hallands Fläder is flavoured with elderflowers. In Alsace, elderflowers are distilled to make *eau de vie* (water of life) spirit. Romanians produce a slightly fermented soft beverage from elderflowers called *socat*. A similar drink is made in the United Kingdom but is allowed to ferment in a closed pressure-proof bottle, resulting in a fizzy alcoholic drink called elderflower champagne.

Elderflower vinegar has been in use for centuries; John Partridge cites a recipe for 'elderne' flower vinegar in his book *The Treasure of Hidden Secrets & Commodious Conceits* (1586). Writing in 1664, the English gardener and writer John Evelyn recommended elderflowers infused in vinegar as a salad ingredient. Elderflowers find their way into many dishes throughout Europe, although a cook must be opportunistic when using the flowers, since they should be harvested when

Elderflower syrup from IKEA (left) and St Germain, an elderflower cordial.

Elderflower fritters with flowers from Norm's Farms.

fully opened but before insects have the chance to pollinate them, a narrow window indeed. Once pollinated, the flowers rapidly lose both their honey-like fragrance and their taste, which is likened to sweet muscat grapes.

Elderflowers are also commonly brewed into a tea, as illustrated in the Hans Christian Andersen story. Roma people gathered elderflowers – after first asking permission of the Elderflower Mother and offering her a prayer – and brewed them into a medicinal tea. Today, Gypsy Cold Medicine, an elderflower tea, can still be found in some retail outlets.

The European taste for elderflowers is gaining popularity in the United States, although 90 per cent of elderflower products used in the u.s. are still imported from Europe. But that is changing; in State College, Pennsylvania, the chef Bernd Brandstatter forages for elderflowers in the spring and makes elderflower fritters for patrons at his family's restaurant, Herwig's Austrian Bistro. Elderflower products, especially syrups, are appearing in retail markets such as IKEA. Norm's Farms in North Carolina sells syrups, dried elderflowers and cuttings in their store and online to encourage elderflower cultivation.

Additional Edible Flowers of Europe

Many other edible flowers are in use throughout Europe. Sorrel (*Rumex acetosella, Rumex scutatus*) is native to Europe and western Asia and the flower has been in culinary usage since the ancient Egyptians. Sorrel adds a tangy tartness to dishes. The lemony, floral flavour of lilac (*Syringa vulgaris*) is a creative addition to marinades and jellies and can also be used as a garnish. The lavender, pink or white flowers may be paired with desserts.

In the fifteenth century primrose (*Oenothera*) pottage was a favourite Easter delicacy. The flower was also used in salads and as sugared sweetmeats. Today, the crystallized flowers are used in a modern custard-based dessert that still goes by the old name of primrose pottage. Widely used in Spain as a salad plant and formerly used in England to flavour wine and vinegars, cowslip (*Primula veris*) 'strengthens the brain and is a preservative against madness', according to *The Gentlewoman's Companion* (1639). Chamomile (*Chamaemelum nobile*) is commonly used as a tea infusion because of its calming, soothing properties. The ancient Egyptians used it to cure fevers and also used chamomile oil in their embalming rituals.

Although the tall, thin stalks of chive (*Allium schoenoprasum, Allium tuberosum*) are more commonly used in cooking, the flowers – called scapes – have culinary utility. Believed to lower blood pressure and reduce cholesterol, among other medicinal properties, the small pinkish-purple balls of tiny

Other edible flowers from Europe. From left to right, beginning at top: sorrel, lilac, primrose, cowslip, chamomile, geranium, chive and clover.

flowers are good in soups, salads, eggs and breads. Scape soup is made from whole flower heads. Charlemagne recommended that his subjects plant chives in their gardens.

A symbol of Ireland and St Patrick, clover (*Trifolium*), especially red clover, has long been used in wine, jellies, teas and to flavour vinegar. The tiny petals have a sweet, aniseed flavour. They can be used in cakes, desserts and salads. Native to South Africa, scented geraniums (*Pelargonium*) were brought back to England by British colonists and used in jellies, cakes, desserts and teas.

7
The Americas

A sixteenth-century statue unearthed on the side of the volcano Popocatépetl in Mexico depicts the Aztec god Xochipilli, whose name means 'flower prince', seated upon a stone pediment. Both the pediment and the god's body are adorned with mushrooms and three different varieties of flowers, all hallucinogenic. The god's head is thrown back, his mouth open; he seems to be in a state of drug-induced ecstasy. R. G. Wasson, an author and ethnomycologist, writes in his book *The Wondrous Mushroom: Mycolatry in Mesoamerica* (1980) that 'He is absorbed in *temicxoch*, "the flowery dream", as the Nahua say in describing the awesome experience that follows the ingestion of sinicuichi (*Heima salicifolia*).'

While the Aztecs and other indigenous peoples of the Americas certainly used a variety of flowers as medicines and sacred hallucinogens, they also incorporated them into their cuisine. One common usage, and again one with sacred connotations, was to add flowers to chocolate (cacao) as a flavouring agent. Chocolate was not an everyday drink but was reserved for sacred occasions and the exclusive use of the ruling class. Chocolate, bitter in its natural state, was rarely served without some flavouring additives, and several different flowers were used for that purpose. The ear-shaped petals of hueinacaztli

Statue of the Aztec god Xochipilli, whose name means 'flower prince'.

(*Cymbopetalum pendulifolorum*) were turned into a powder and added to the cacao; it was said that too much of the flower could lead to drunkenness. A second flower used in chocolate was mecaxochitl (*Piper sanctum*). Magnolia flowers (*Magnolia mexicana*) could also be mixed into the drink. Vanilla was a common additive as well, although the pods were used rather than the flowers. Cacaoxochitl flower was also a chocolate flavouring additive, called in Spanish *flor del cacao*, and is still used that way by indigenous people in Mexico.

Squash

A wide variety of squashes and other members of the *Cucurbita* family were found throughout the Americas by the time of European contact. Native to and first cultivated in the Andes and Mesoamerica, squash eventually spread into North America where it was often planted along with corn and beans, under the umbrella term 'three sisters', creating a perfectly balanced and efficient diet. Everywhere squash was cultivated, the seeds, flesh and flowers of the plants found their way into the local cuisine.

In his book, *Observations on the Inhabitants, Climate, Soil, Rivers, Productions, Animals, and Other Matters Worthy of Notice Made By Mr John Bartram*, published in London in 1751, the Philadelphia botanist John Bartram recounted a dinner he had while on a trip to upstate New York where he visited the Onondaga, one of the Five Nations of the Iroquois Confederacy. Among the dishes served to him was 'one kettle full of young squashes, their flowers boiled in water and a little meal mixed'. Apparently it was not to Bartram's Eurocentric liking, as he wrote: 'This dish was but weak food.'

Further west and in the southwest, Indian tribes fried squash blossoms, ate them fresh, used them as soup flavourings or added them to salads. In fact, squash blossoms were a common indigenous delicacy throughout the Americas. Many flower blossoms are produced per vine, allowing plenty to be picked while still leaving enough to mature and ensure a supply of winter produce. The squash blossom has a taste similar to the vegetable itself, although it is sweeter and a little more delicate.

As European explorers traversed the Americas, they sent seeds and plants of squash back home. Europeans were slow to include these strange new vegetables in their cuisines, although pumpkins and squashes were valued for their medicinal properties. A painting by Vincenzo Campi titled *The Fruit Seller* of 1580 indicates that Italians ate squash blossoms then as they still do now.

Today, squash blossoms are found in a variety of dishes in the southwestern United States and in Mexico. Fresh blossoms may be stuffed with cheese, corn, chillies, couscous, bread crumbs or other ingredients, then battered and deep-fried. The blossoms may also be chopped and blended into salads and soups. Squash blossoms are also used in quesadillas, scrambled eggs, omelettes and in a pork or beef stew called *chimoie*. Other common uses include featuring the blossoms in fritters, soufflés, burritos and Indian pudding.

Squash blossoms in a French market.

Marigolds

Although Spanish explorers to the Americas thought they had 'discovered' the culinary and medicinal benefits of the marigolds (genus *Tagetes*) that they found growing in these regions, the indigenous peoples had known about them for centuries.

There are several different flowers commonly known as 'marigolds' that belong to distinct genera: *Bidens tripartita*, *Caltha palustris*, *Calendula officinalis* and the genus *Tagetes*. The last are hardy annual flowers that occur in brilliant hues of yellow, gold, orange, mahogany and sometimes red or white. These marigolds are indigenous to the American Southwest and to Central and South America and were subsequently spread throughout the rest of the world by early colonists returning to Europe.

The Incas of Peru made a potato dish called *ocopa* that was used as a travelling ration for their fleet-footed messengers. The dish has evolved over the centuries and is now a speciality of the city of Arequipa in the mountains of southern Peru. A key ingredient in the dish is a paste that includes *huacatay*, marigolds of the genus *Tagetes minuta*. These marigolds are also used as herbs in dishes from Bolivia, Chile and Ecuador and are often described as tasting like a mixture of sweet basil, mint and tarragon, with a hint of citrus. The flowers may also be brewed into a medicinal tea; in Mexico, a sweet anise-flavoured medicinal tea called *pericón* is brewed from marigolds (*Tagetes lucida*) and here, too, marigolds are used as a culinary herb, often as a substitute for tarragon.

The wild marigolds *Tagetes erecta*, known more commonly as Mexican mint marigold, grow 3 to 4 ft (1 m) high and just as wide, and are native to Mexico and Guatemala. They have flowers that are 2 to 4 in. (5–10 cm) across and are very fragrant. The plant has been used for centuries as a beverage, dye

Marigolds being sold as prayer flowers in an Indian grocery in Singapore. In addition to being edible, marigolds have been used in religious ceremonies by various cultures around the world.

and flavouring as well as medicinally. Mexican mint marigold has many other aliases, most alluding to its fragrance: sweet mace, Mexican or winter tarragon, sweet- or mint-scented marigold, root beer plant and yerba anis.

The leaves have also been used medicinally in folk remedies for malaria, colic and colds, and a poultice made from marigold leaves is a traditional treatment for rattlesnake bites. The Tarahumara of Chihuahua and the Huichol of Jalisco and Nayarit especially favour this herb and use it in their religious rituals. According to legend, the ancient Aztec chieftains used a powder made from the aromatic leaves of mint marigold to calm the hapless victims of sacrificial rituals. The Aztecs also used it to flavour *chocolatl*, a foaming, cocoa-based drink.

Marigolds are sometimes called *flor de muerto*, flower of death, and symbolize pain and grief. Every year on the first and second days of November, the indigenous peoples of

Mexico relive a little of their past with the Día de los Muertos or Day of the Dead celebration, a festival that has its roots in Mexico's ancient pre-Hispanic times. Altars of various sizes are set up with food and drinks as offerings to the spirits of deceased family members who, it is believed, return once again on those days to visit with their families and friends. No altar is ever complete without gathering wild marigolds and

Traditional Mexican Day of the Dead altar. Shining marigolds light the way for departed souls to return to earth. Special breads are made with orange-blossom water (centre bottom).

spreading them everywhere from the family altar to pathways and streets, and even throughout cemeteries.

Upon the arrival of the Spanish explorers in the early sixteenth century, the marigold, and its inherent colours, took on a whole new significance. The rich yellow or orange colour of *Tagetes erecta* is accentuated by splashes of red. The flower became a living symbol of the Spanish massacre of the indigenous people: the red blood of the Aztecs splashed over the yellow gold that the Spanish stole from them.

In North America, Dutch settlers were some of the earliest cooks to use marigold in their kitchens. But the marigold they used was actually calendula, also called 'pot marigold', a flower native to Asia and southern Europe. According to Cathy Wilkinson Barash, writing in *Edible Flowers: From Garden to Palate* (1995), European settlers in America brought calendula with them. In the seventeenth century the Dutch were renowned as horticulturalists and experimented in creating new varieties of numerous flowers, many of which found their way into Dutch kitchens; *The Sensible Cook*, a Dutch cookbook, contains a recipe for a lettuce salad that also uses bugloss, borage, rose and pot marigold (*Calendula officinalis*). 'Pot marigold' was shortened to 'marigold', confusing readers about which flower the writer was discussing, calendula or true marigold (any of the *Tagetes*).

Modern cooks use marigolds in a variety of ways. Fresh, the petals can be added to salads and soups or as a complement to squash, cheese dip and fish dishes, for example. For those with a sweet tooth, marigolds can be baked into cakes or covered in sugar, and the petals are pretty toppings for cakes and cupcakes. The petals can also be steeped into a tea using 1 teaspoon of dried petals in 240 ml (8 ounces) of hot water.

Hibiscus

In various places around the world, hibiscus is consumed as food or is added to food and drinks as a flavouring agent. The flowers and calyces (collectively, the sepals, the outermost whorl of parts that form a flower) may be eaten cooked, raw or pickled, and also used as a spice or food dye. The calyces have a mild, tart, citrus taste and can be used for anything that a citrus flavour would pair with, such as rum drinks, fruity or spicy cakes, or even meat dressings and *moles*.

In the Americas, especially the Caribbean and Central and South America, hibiscus calyces find their way into a variety of culinary specialities. The chef Oscar Carrizosa sells hibiscus blended into chocolate tablets at his Casa Crespo restaurant in Oaxaca, Mexico. The resulting 'chocolate Jamaica' is then used in water or hot milk as a drink. The Mexican chef Ricardo Muñoz Zurita, of Azul Restaurantes, invented an unusual vegetarian dish, in part to support the indigenous people of Oaxaca who grow and harvest hibiscus. Instead of the traditional enchilada meat stuffing of chicken or beef, Muñoz Zurita uses hibiscus calyces, giving the dish a meaty, tangy flavour. Hibiscus stalks are sometimes added to soups in Central America to give them this same meaty flavour. Oaxaca is also famous for its many different *moles*, including some that combine hibiscus with pecans or ancho chillies.

In Mexico, hibiscus is used to make *agua fresca*, an inexpensive beverage typically made from fresh juices or extracts, as well as hot tea. For tea, the calyx is steeped or boiled, depending on the recipe, and sugar is added. Ginger, cloves, cinnamon and nutmeg are used in some areas of Mexico to flavour the tea or *agua fresca*. Dried hibiscus is edible and considered a delicacy in Mexico. The calyces may

The fiery red calyces of a hibiscus plant.

also be sweetened and used as a garnish or a sweet appetizer when stuffed with cream cheese, Gournay or some other soft cheese.

Dried hibiscus calyces, often labelled *flor de Jamaica*, have long been available in health food stores in the United States for making hibiscus tea, especially in California and other areas influenced by Mexican customs. *Flor de Jamaica* has a reputation for being a mild natural diuretic. Hibiscus tea (an infusion) is popular all around the world. In the United States, hibiscus tea was popularized by Celestial Seasonings as 'Red Zinger' in 1972. As well as being a natural diuretic, hibiscus tea has lots of vitamin C. There is also at least one u.s. government study that shows that hibiscus tea lowers blood pressure. The Caribbean Development Company, a Trinidad and Tobago brewery, produces a sorrel shandy in which the tea is combined with beer.

In Jamaica, a dash of rum will probably also be added to *agua de Jamaica*, a hibiscus infusion. The drink is stirred and served chilled and is a Christmas tradition in Jamaica, served along with fruit cake or potato pudding. In Panama both the hibiscus flowers and the drink are called *saril* (a derivative of the English word 'sorrel'). The drink is prepared by picking and boiling the calyces with chopped ginger, sugar, clove, cinnamon and nutmeg and it is also traditionally drunk at Christmas.

The ancestors of today's modern hibiscus hybrids were originally native to Mauritius, Madagascar, Fiji, Hawaii and either China or India. Trade routes distributed hibiscus to warm, tropical lands all around the globe, following the Equator. Hibiscus is brewed into tea, or served as a cold beverage in much of Africa, including Ghana, Senegal, Mali, Burkina Faso, the Ivory Coast, Sudan and Egypt. The hibiscus calyces are also harvested in these countries as a food source and may be consumed cooked or made into a sour sauce. In addition to domestic consumption, hibiscus exports have been an important source of income for West African farmers.

Nasturtium

While most edible flowers have a subtle flavour, nasturtiums surprise the palate with their strong, peppery taste. The word 'nasturtium' is derived from two Latin words, *nasus*, meaning 'nose', and *tortus*, meaning 'twisted or tortured'. The two words together designate something that tortures the nose as would a plant with an unexpectedly strong and unusual smell. The flowers and buds exude an intense flavour and the young leaves are tender and edible as well. Nasturtiums are popular with chefs and home gardeners because their colourful flowers not only dress up a plate, but are high in vitamins A, C (ten times as much as lettuce) and D. In the world of edible annual flowers, nasturtiums are one of the tastiest and easiest to grow. Nasturtiums grow quickly from seed and, depending on the variety, can be grown as climbers on fences and trellises or as bushy plants in window boxes and containers.

The garden nasturtiums commonly grown today descend mainly from two species native to Peru. The first, brought to Europe by Spanish conquistadors in the late fifteenth and early sixteenth centuries, was *Tropaeolum minus*, a semi-trailing vine bearing spurred, lightly scented orange-yellow flowers with dark red spots on the petals and shield-shaped leaves. In the late seventeenth century, a Dutch botanist introduced the taller, more vigorous *Tropaeolum majus*, a trailing vine with darker orange flowers and more rounded leaves. Since Spanish and Dutch herbalists shared seeds with their counterparts, the pretty, fragrant and easy-to-grow plants quickly became widespread throughout Europe and Britain. In the eighteenth century, nasturtiums were introduced into North America by European settlers who brought seeds from home to be planted in the new land. These sometimes went by the names

Henri Fantin-Latour, *Nasturtiums*, 1880.

Indian cress and Capuchin cress because the shape of the flowers was reminiscent of a Capuchin monk's hood.

Spanish conquistadores in Central and South America noted that the indigenous peoples they encountered often ate flowers, including nasturtiums. According to Jesuit missionaries, the Incas used nasturtiums as a salad vegetable and as a medicinal herb. In *Forgotten Art of Flower Cookery* (1973), Leona Woodring Smith notes that nasturtiums from the Americas were mentioned in a sixteenth-century Spaniard's book about discoveries in the 'New Found World'.

Although the Philadelphia seedsman Bernard McMahon has often been credited with the wholesale introduction of nasturtiums into the United States in the early nineteenth century – he lists nasturtium as an 'esculent' (edible) plant in his seed list of 1803 – there are earlier reports of nasturtiums being cultivated in the country. Thomas Jefferson recorded planting 'Nasturcium', along with 'Cresses, Celery, and Radichio', on 26 March 1774, in a meadow of his Monticello estate, supporting the popular use of nasturtiums as an edible plant, either by pickling its seeds and flower buds (much like capers) or by using its leaves in salads. Later, however, Jefferson listed nasturtiums with other ornamental plants in a 'Calendar of the bloom of flowers in 1782' and showed it blooming from July until the end of September. In 1824 Mary Randolph, a first cousin of Jefferson's from Richmond, Virginia, published *The Virginia Housewife*, considered by food historians to be one of the most influential cookbooks of the nineteenth century. Many of the book's recipes are also found among the surviving papers of Jefferson's daughter, Martha, and his granddaughters, suggesting an exchange of culinary ideas between the families. One recipe in the book describes how to pickle nasturtiums:

> Gather the berries when full grown but young, put them in a pot, pour boiling salt and water on, and let them stand three or four days; then drain off the water, and cover them with cold vinegar; add a few blades of mace, and whole grains of black pepper.

Nasturtiums taste somewhat like spicy watercress (the botanical name for watercress is *Nasturtium officinale*). Nasturtium leaves can be added to any type of green salad or even sprinkled into soups; President Dwight D. Eisenhower was renowned for his hearty vegetable soup, which included nasturtium. When mixed with chives, both the leaves and blossoms of the flower blend beautifully into omelettes or potato salad.

Isabella Stewart Gardner, a wealthy nineteenth-century patron of the arts, made sure nasturtiums were prominent at her Boston art museum. She often hung the plants to coincide with the opening of the museum the week before the Easter holiday. Nasturtium vines are grown from seeds sown in late summer and are intensively cultivated in the Gardner Museum greenhouses throughout the winter in preparation for the spring display. For over a century, the tradition of hanging nasturtiums from the balconies of the museum's Venetian courtyard has been a reliable predictor of spring. Moreover, the museum's Café G also highlights the edible flower on its menu each spring with seasonal menu items.

Other Edible Flowers of the Americas

Many other edible flowers can be found in the cuisines of the Americas. Flor de Izote (*Yucca guatemalensis*) should not be confused with the root crop yucca. These yucca flowers are rich in vitamins and minerals. Indigenous people of Central America eat the flower buds of various species of yucca. The buds are slightly spicy and have an acid taste disagreeable to some palates. They are often added to salads or cooked with eggs and potatoes.

Canadian honewort (*Cryptotaenia canadensis*) is a member of the carrot family and is common in two-thirds of eastern North America, growing as far south as Florida. Also known as wild chervil, the entire plant is edible. The small blossoms are cooked and added to salads for their aromatic quality.

The lovely flower petals of banana passion fruit (*Passiflora*) are edible, and particularly tasty in salads. As with all edibles, the stamens must be removed or, if used as a garnish, must be served to savvy diners who will remove them on the

Other edible flowers from America. From left to right, beginning at top: flor de izote, Canadian honewort, banana passion fruit, loroco, eastern redbud, magnolia, bird's tongue and sweet goldenrod.

plate. It is a favourite of the Andean people and can be found in the wild in highland valleys in Bolivia, Venezuela, Colombia and Peru. Found primarily in El Salvador, but common to other countries of Central America and Mexico, loroco (*Fernaldia pandurata*) is a flowering plant that is popular in *pupusas,* a traditional dish similar to a grilled or toasted cheese sandwich made from two fresh tortillas with a filling of loroco and cheese in the middle. The buds and unopened flowers are also cooked with cheese, eggs, rice or chicken and can be found in crepes, tortillas and tamales. Fresh loroco is not yet available in the U.S., pending approval by the USDA's Commodity and Biological Risk Analysis. It can, however, be purchased in jars or frozen.

Eastern redbud (*Cercis Canadensis*) can be found throughout much of the United States and Canada. The pretty pinkish-red buds are one of the first signs of spring. Native Americans ate redbud flowers raw or cooked, and also the young pods and seeds. The flowers can be pickled and used in salads or as a condiment, and unopened buds may be pickled as a substitute for capers.

Not many people know that the beautiful, showy flowers of the magnolia tree (*Magnolia grandiflora*), ubiquitous in the southern United States, are edible. Only the petals are used. They are never consumed raw; instead, they are pickled using a sweet-sour recipe, then diced and used sparingly – they have a strong flavour – as a salad flavouring.

The thin, pod-like red scarlet flowers of the colorín tree, also known as bird's tongue, have been eaten in Mexico since pre-colonial times. After cleaning, the flowers are boiled with salt and a small piece of volcanic stone which helps to keep the colour bright. They are often mixed with egg and cheese and fried in oil to create egg pancakes.

While the Boston Tea Party of 1773 eventually led to an independent United States, it also resulted in a shortage of tea. Thankfully, the flowers and leaves of sweet goldenrod (*Solidago odora*) can be made into a tea that tastes like anise – the Revolutionary patriots of the time used it in their substitute 'liberty tea'.

Wasabi flowers.

Afterword

At Chef's Garden, in Huron, Ohio, the farmer Lee Jones snapped off a tiny white flower from its stem. He held it up to us to smell and asked, 'Do you know what this is?' We looked at each other, eyes wide with surprise, thrilled that *yes*, we did know what it was! Just one month previously, and 8,000 miles away, the farmer Bob Allen of Golden Garden in Dalat, Vietnam, had picked the same blossom, asking us the same question with equal enthusiasm for something new in the market of edible flowers. We have no doubt that wasabi flower will be a global hit in this exciting culinary corner. Like the distinct savoury notes of the nasturtium, the tiny, delicate, white wasabi flowers pack an unexpected peppery punch.

Undoubtedly, one of the thrills of preparing this book has been the travel that we did in the name of research (our jealous friends have put that word in air-quotes). From Laos to Mexico, France to Turkey, visiting markets, farms, factories and stores has brought the history of edible flowers alive for us and hopefully for readers as well. The ability to conduct research on the Internet and follow the complex history of each edible flower has taken us down countless 'rabbit holes', as we called them. We got delightfully lost discovering new and fascinating facts about edible flowers. We uncovered sources of information that are available to anyone and everyone. We had fun experimenting with imaginative edible flower recipes. And we have found out that there are lots of people with a curiosity and interest in this field of culinary exploration, which points to a bright future for edible flowers.

Precautions When Eating Edible Flowers

> . . . since the thing perhaps is to eat flowers and not to be afraid
>
> e e cummings

That may be an odd quote to introduce precautions about eating flowers, but it does seem that we are sometimes overly cautious about what we eat. The forager and natural foods proponent Euell Gibbons once said that the most commonly asked question he received from interviewers was, 'Aren't you afraid to eat that?' When did we become so afraid? Was it when we started thinking that everything had to be labelled as 'safe'? Is it because so much of our food is sprayed with toxins that we started to believe the food itself is toxic?

It's not so easy to divide flowers into a neat list of edible and inedible types. Consider the old adage by Paracelsus, 'the dose makes the poison', implying that so many things, when taken in excess, can be toxic. Many flowers have phytochemicals that can be toxic in too great a quantity. As an example, apple blossom may contain a cyanide precursor.

We know from herbal folklore that flowers can be medicinal – and medicine can be 'toxic' if it is not administered in the proper quantities for a particular ailment. The foxglove flower was used medicinally by ancient Romans and was known by the tenth century in Europe for treating heart failure. Indeed, we find that foxglove contains the chemical substance digitalis that today is manufactured by drug companies to treat heart conditions. Drug manufacturers today control the process in order to get a pure calibrated product that doctors can accurately prescribe for a patient. No one should try to treat themselves with foxglove, and as a precaution, it has been included in all lists of inedible flowers.

Other flowers are not clearly identifiable as either edible or inedible. For example, azaleas are not recognized as safe to eat in the United States, or most parts of the world for that matter, yet people in North Korea have eaten them; several children died as a result. Paradoxically, Korean women cooked and ate azaleas with rice – apparently without ill effects – in the traditional Korean festival of Samjinnal. Perhaps a different species of azalea grows in Korea.

Hibiscus tea can act as a mild diuretic, but so can watermelon and yet we do not consider watermelon toxic. Sweet woodruff can have a blood-thinning effect if taken in large quantities. Of all the varieties of begonias, it is only the *Tuberosa begonia* petals that are edible, and even those should be eaten in moderation and not consumed by people suffering from gout, kidney stones or rheumatism. Some flowers, such as daylilies, can have a laxative effect in some individuals if taken in too large a quantity and may cause diarrhoea.

Some people are allergic to the pollen in certain flowers. As an example, people who have hay fever or asthma may be particularly susceptible to an allergic reaction caused by eating members of the daisy family. The possibility of an allergic reaction among some people has caused certain flowers to be included on the inedible list, yet we don't generally classify peanuts as inedible just because some people are allergic to them. Often people who have other food allergies are allergic to some flower pollens. To reduce the likelihood of a pollen allergic reaction, the flower's stamens (the pollen-producing part of the flower) are often removed and the flower washed to remove the pollen before the flower is used as food. Pollen purchased in health food stores should be used sparingly until it is established that there is no individual allergic reaction.

Some flowers, like orchids, may technically be edible in that they will not make you sick, but they may not taste particularly pleasant – or have no discernible taste at all. The taste of snapdragons is often described as bland. Of course, taste differs among individuals. Most guidelines recommend cutting off the base of the individual petals as that often tastes bitter. However, as noted in *Bitter: A Taste of the World's Most Dangerous Flavors, with Recipes* (2014) by Jennifer McLagan, small amounts of a bitter taste (think rocket (arugula) or radicchio) can be intriguing and add complexity to a dish.

While our ancestors would have been capable of identifying many plants, modern man seems to have lost that knowledge. We can help rectify this by referring to well researched books such as Euell Gibbons's *Handbook of Edible Wild Plants*. We can also learn about foraging first-hand through foraging 'meetups', like Wild Foodies in Philadelphia, and demonstrations like those conducted by the naturalist Steve 'Wildman' Brill, the New York City 'Central Park Forager', who gained notoriety in 1986 when he was arrested in Central Park for picking and eating a dandelion. Be cautious about using old herbal sources which may contain outdated information and certainly do not experiment upon yourself. Shennong, the legendary father of Chinese medicine, reputedly catalogued 365 species of medicinal plants but died when he ate the yellow flower of an unknown weed which caused his intestines to rupture.

Although Euell Gibbons maintained that there wasn't a single rule of thumb that could be applied to flowers to determine whether or not they were safe to eat, there are some general guidelines that should be observed. Use only flowers that you can confidently identify and know are edible (see resources for lists). Some people say elderflowers and Queen Anne's lace, both of which are edible, look like hemlock, which is poisonous – remember how Socrates died. Be aware that taxonomy is important. As an example; daylilies (genus *Hemerocallidoideae*) are edible, but other lilies are not.

Make sure the flowers have not been sprayed with pesticides. Flowers from florists will almost certainly have been sprayed with pesticides and should not be eaten. Cut flowers may contain up to fifty times the pesticides and fungicides permitted on food crops. Also, it is possible that those flowers may have been imported from countries with lax environmental regulations, and, since imported flowers are required to be pest-free, they may be saturated with chemicals before reaching your local florist.

Use only flowers that have not been exposed to environmental pollution, such as contaminated water, automobile exhaust or lead-based paint. This precaution is a difficult one to enforce but also points out the importance of organic gardening as a safe and environmentally friendly way to raise flowers and vegetables.

It is important to remember to be considerate when foraging for edible flowers. Do not forage on private property without permission and do so carefully, so as to cause as little damage as possible to the environment. Do not forage any endangered flower varieties. Also, when canning or preserving edible flowers in jams, jellies, sugars and other such methods, ensure you follow all the proper, recommended procedures to avoid contamination (such as botulism) in the final product.

Any item placed on a person's plate should be edible. DO NOT garnish Christmas dinners with a beautiful yet inedible poinsettia – it can cause mouth irritation and vomiting! A much better choice would be a lightly sautéed sprig of sage flowers. Not only would this be pretty and delicious, but a garnish such as this signals and brings out the taste of the seasoning that is in the turkey stuffing.

The song 'Please Don't Eat the Daisies', sung by Doris Day in the movie of the same name, was really just about her mischievous boys eating the centrepiece of daisies before an important dinner party. It is possible to eat daisies and many other flowers as well. This book has only touched upon a few of the many edible flowers. For a more complete listing of edible flowers in your area and those that should be avoided, you can contact your county agricultural extension agent or consult several websites including the seed supplier Thompson (see Websites and Associations).

We have tried to include the most accurate, complete and up-to-date information in this book, but we also encourage our readers to explore and discover more about edible flowers on their own. The information in this book is intended for educational purposes only and should not be considered as a recommendation or an endorsement of any particular medical or health treatment.

Flower Dinner Menu

Early in our research for this book, we were delighted to learn of an 'Edible Flower Luncheon and Garden Tour' at the historic Hartwood Mansion near Pittsburgh. Not long afterwards, while we were again enjoying our research into edible flowers in Oaxaca, Mexico, we came upon a lovely description in Adela Fernandez's cookbook, *Traditional Mexican Cooking*, of an impressive courtship dinner her father once prepared for his beloved using edible flowers in each dish. The chef Alice Waters describes a beautiful 'Dinner of Flowers' in her book *The Chez Panisse Menu Cookbook*, listed in the chapter aptly titled 'Memorable Menus'.

We invite you to create your own memorable flower-power menu with suggestions below for each course. You might try a meal of several courses created around one special flower or maybe just one fabulously memorable dish like the rose petal sauce on quail dish sensuously portrayed in the film version of Laura Esquivel's novel *Like Water for Chocolate*. Edible flower recipes abound on the Internet and there are even chef consultants whose job entails creating imaginative menus using edible flowers.

Cocktails

Wine with borage flower floating in it
Syrups or cordials with flower components (Chartreuse, crème
de Yvette, Mai Tai, St Germain or Ramos Gin Fizz)

Hibiscus punch (non-alcoholic alternative) served in a punch
bowl with an ice ring of flowers or flowers in ice cubes

Starters

Devilled eggs garnished with flowers and capers
Artichokes
Cheese (flowers pressed into cheese)
Stuffed nasturtiums, hibiscus or squash blossoms
Bruschetta with cheese and flowers sprinkled in and topped
with pea, fava bean, borage, chive, basil, wasabi or mustard
green flowers

Salad

Greens with lots of flowers (nasturtiums, marigolds and more)
and dressed with a flower-infused vinegar
Banana flower salad
Moroccan orange salad (orange-blossom water and rose petals)
Lavender or elderflower sorbet between courses

Soup

Squash soup with fried squash blossom as a garnish (other petals
sprinkled on top, such as borage, rocket (arugula), sage or thyme
flowers) Chinese hot and sour soup with 'golden threads' (daylilies)

Main courses

(plate decorated with edible flowers
as a garnish)
Chicken piccata with capers
Pork roast with Herbes de Provence rub
Chicken bastilla (orange-blossom water)
Flower hotpot (with lotus, daylily pods and
bolting Chinese vegetables)
Quesadilla with lorocco flowers
Moo shu pork with 'golden threads' (daylilies)

Side dishes

Saffron rice
Broccoli and green buds of broccoli rabe
Chinese vegetables 'bolted'
Artichoke mushroom risotto
Herbes de Provence scalloped potatoes
Sautéed daylily pods or squash blossoms
French bread with flower butter

Wine

Elderflower and/or dandelion wine
Chrysanthemum wine

Dessert

Assortment of tea cakes decorated with candied violets
and pansies

Assortment of Indian or Persian rosewater sweets such
as *gulab jamun* and *faloodeh*
Assortment of sweet goods such as violet candy
and lavender chocolates
Marigold scones with fairy butter or rose-petal jam
Lavender crème brûlée, panna cotta or brownies
Tuberous citrus begonias with yoghurt dip
Berries with elderflower or honeysuckle syrup

After-dinner drinks

Wine, as mentioned above
Tea (there are dozens of teas made with dried flowers,
for example, lotus tea)
Coffee (white coffee made with orange-blossom water
or Arabian coffee with saffron)

Recipes

Aliter Ius in Avibus (Another Sauce for Fowl)
from Apicius, *Cookery and Dining in Imperial Rome*, ed. and trans. Joseph
Dommers Vehling (New York, 1977)

Pepper, lovage, parsley, dry mint, fennel blossoms moistened with
wine; add roasted nuts from pontus [Turkish hazelnuts] or almonds,
a little honey, wine, vinegar, and broth to taste. Put oil in a pot,
and heat and stir the sauce, adding green celery seeds, cat-mint;
carve the fowl and cover with the sauce.

Conserve of Roses
from Hannah Woolley, *The Gentlewoman's Companion* (1675)

Take red-Rose-buds, clip all the white, either bruised or withered
from them; then add to every pound of Roses, three pound of
Sugar, stamp the Roses very small, putting to them a little juice of
Lemons or Rose-water as they become dry; when you think your
Roses small enough, then put your Sugar to them, so beat them
together till they be well mingled, then put it up in Gally-pots or
Glasses. In this manner is made the Conserve of Flowers of
Violets, which doth cool and open in a burning Fever or Ague,
being dissolved in Almond-milk, and so taken; and excellent good
for any inflammation in Children.

Thus you may also make the Conserve of Cowslips, which
strengthens the brain, and is a Preservative against Madness; it

helps the Memory, asswageth the pain of the head, and helpeth most infirmities thereof. In like manner you may also make Conserve of Marigolds, which taken fasting in the morning is very good against Melancholy; cureth the trembling of the heart, and very good against any Pestilential distemper.

Blamanger
from Robert May, *The Accomplisht Cook* (1685)

Take a capon being boil'd or rosted & mince it small then have a pound of blanched almonds beaten to a paste, and beat the minced capon amongst it, with some rose-water, mingle it with some cream, ten whites of eggs, and grated manchet [wheat bread], strain all the foresaid things with some salt, sugar, and a little musk [monkey flower], boil them in a pan or broad skillet clean scowred as thick as pap, in the boiling stir it continually, being boil'd strain it again, and serve it in paste in the foregoing forms, or made dishes with paste royal.

To make your paste for the forms, take to a quart of flour a quarter of a pound of butter, and the yolks of four eggs, boil your butter in fair water, and put the yolks of the eight eggs on one side of your dish, make up your paste quick, not too dry, and make it stiff.

Fairy Butter

Fairy butter, also called orange butter, was popular both in England and America in the eighteenth century. Dolly Madison served it in the White House and Elizabeth Cleland included it in her 1759 *Receipt Book*. The following recipe is from Maria Eliza Rundell's 1807 cookbook, *A New System of Domestic Cookery*.

Boil six eggs hard. Beat the yolks in a mortar with fine sugar, orange flower water, four ounces of butter and two ounces of almonds beaten to a paste. When all is mixed, rub it through a colander on a dish.

14th of July Salad
Adapted from *The Alice B. Toklas Cook Book* (New York, 1954)

Alice B. Toklas served this salad to commemorate Bastille Day,
14 July. It includes capers and nasturtiums, both edible flowers.

2 cups (440 g) mayonnaise
½ cup (120 g) capers
½ cup (120 g) chopped dill pickles
1 lb (450 g) deboned white fish (or albacore tuna)
1 pinch saffron

Mix the ingredients and serve with a salad of nasturtium leaves
and cucumbers with a dressing of olive oil and garlic mixed with
tarragon vinegar. Garnish the dish with orange and red nasturtiums.

Salads are an easy place for the cook to add edible flowers to a
dish. Marigold petals, violets and borage flowers are very attractive
in salads. Garnishing with borage flowers, which have a slight
cucumber taste, would complement the cucumber in this salad.
Serves 4

Beef with Rosebuds
Adapted from Lilia Zaouali,
Medieval Cuisine of the Islamic World
(Los Angeles, CA, 2007)

½ pound (225 g) stewing beef, cubed
1 tbsp olive oil
1 onion, sliced
1 tbsp dried rosebuds, crushed
1 lemon, juiced
2 tsp ground black pepper
2 tsp cinnamon
¼ tsp mastic (optional)
1 cup (240 ml) beef stock (broth)

Meat was usually blanched (dropped into boiling water for a minute or two) in the Middle Ages. Modern cooks may want to skip this step and sauté the beef cubes in a tablespoon of olive oil along with the sliced onions.

When the onions have softened, add pepper, lemon juice, cinnamon and rosebuds. Add the mastic if you have it available. If not, an alternative is to add a tablespoon of toasted pine nuts as a garnish to the final dish as mastic has a somewhat 'piney' taste.

An alternative to the spices listed in the ingredients is to purchase advieh, a spice mixture used in Persian cuisine which is available from ethnic and specialty spice shops. Advieh is a mixture of crushed rose buds, black pepper and cinnamon, sometimes with other spices added.

Add the stock and simmer for 30 minutes.

Serves 4

Havasupai Indian Squash Blossom Pudding
Adapted from Cathy Wilkinson Barash, *Edible Flowers: Desserts and Drinks* (Golden, CO, 1977)

kernels from 3 ears of green corn
2 to 3 cups (100–150 g) squash blossoms, destemmed
salt to taste

Green corn is very young ears of sweet corn. If green corn is not available, you can substitute 2 cups (290 g) of white corn kernels. Place the corn in a saucepan, adding just enough water to cover it. Cook over medium-low heat for half an hour. In another saucepan, place the squash blossoms. Cover with water, bring to a boil and cook until tender. Drain the blossoms and mash. Stir the mashed blossoms into green corn and continue to cook until thickened. Salt to taste.

Serves 4–6

Violet Pineapple Soup

Adapted from Leona Woodring Smith,

The Forgotten Art of Flower Cookery (New York, 1973)

3 cups (720 ml) pineapple juice
2 tbsp quick-cooking tapioca
juice from one lemon
½ tsp lemon zest
2 cups (300 g) sliced strawberries or red
raspberries
1 cup (150 g) diced orange sections, or drained
canned mandarin sections
2 tbsp orange liqueur (optional)
2 tbsp sour cream
½ cup (25 g) fresh violets

Combine the pineapple juice, lemon juice, lemon zest and tapioca and bring to a boil. Cool to room temperature. Add the fruit, orange liqueur and violets and blend. Chill. Before serving, top each bowl with sour cream and a fresh violet.

Serves 4–6

Rose Petal Sorbet

Adapted from Rosalind Creasy, *The Edible Flower Garden*

(Boston, MA, 1999)

¾ cup (180 g) rose syrup
3 cups (720 ml) white grape juice
juice of one lemon

While Creasy recommends using a late harvest Gewürztraminer grape juice, a reasonable substitute is white grape juice with lemon.

A day before serving, combine the syrup and grape juice in an ice cream maker. Follow the manufacturer's directions for making sorbet. Once the sorbet is done, freeze it in an airtight container for 24 hours.

Creasy recommends serving the sorbet in a rose. To serve, choose four perfect large roses and remove the centres. Spread the petals open and secure them to the middle of the plates or dishes with a bit of egg white. Just before serving, place a scoop of sorbet in each rose.

A flower sorbet similar to this one can be made with a variety of flower syrups. Flower syrups can purchased in speciality stores in flavours such as elderflower, lavender, saffron, honeysuckle and hibiscus. Asian groceries may have additional flavours such as kewda (flowers from the pandanus plant). You could also make your own flower syrups by adding flower-flavoured waters or bitters (such as orange blossom water) to a simple syrup (one part sugar to one part water, bring to boil until sugar has dissolved, then allow to cool before you add the flower water).

While Creasy described presenting the sorbet in an opened rose, other edible flowers, such as tulips, daylilies and nasturtiums, can also be used as pretty containers. Just be sure to remove the pistils and stamens from the inside of the flower.

Sage-flower Mustard
Adapted from Kathy Brown, *The Edible Flower Garden* (Leicester, 2011)

2 tbsp sage flowers, all green parts removed
4 tbsp crème fraîche
¼ tsp English mustard powder
1 tbsp young sage leaves
1 tbsp garlic chive leaves

Carefully remove each sage flower from its socket. Discard any that are damaged. Combine the crème fraîche and mustard powder. Finely shred and cut the sage leaves and garlic chive leaves into small segments and add to the mixture. Toss lightly together and add the sage flowers.

The flowers of many herbs can be substituted in this recipe. For example, chive blossoms and thyme flowers could be substituted for the sage blossoms or added along with the sage blossoms.

Hibiscus Chutney

Adapted from Miche Bacher, *Cooking with Flowers*
(Philadelphia, PA, 2013)

2 pints (340 g) fresh blackberries
8 hibiscus flowers in syrup, chopped
½ cup (75 g) red onion, finely chopped
1 jalapeño pepper, seeded and chopped
2 tbsp minced fresh ginger
2 tbsp Dijon mustard
salt and pepper to taste (optional)
½ cup (120 ml) white wine vinegar

Hibiscus flowers in syrup can be purchased in jars. Alternatively, you can place dried hibiscus flowers in equal parts of water and sugar and boil down to a syrup.

Put all the ingredients except the vinegar into a saucepan. Cook and occasionally stir the mixture over medium heat for about 5 minutes. Add salt and pepper to taste. Stir in the vinegar and let the mixture simmer and thicken for about 10 minutes more. This chutney will last for up to 6 weeks when refrigerated in an airtight container.

Moo Shu Pork

This recipe calls for 'golden needles', which are dried lily buds. Chinese folklore says that tying the golden needles in a knot keeps the spirit of the flower inside. However, there is a more practical reason: tying the buds prevents them from disintegrating during cooking.

½ lb (225 g) lean pork, cut into julienne shreds
¼ cup (25 g) dried Chinese wood ear mushrooms
½ cup (25 g) golden needles
3 eggs, beaten
1 tbsp rice wine vinegar

2 tbsp soy sauce
1 tsp cornflour (cornstarch)
3 tbsp oil
1 tbsp grated fresh ginger root
1 spring onion (scallion), shredded
hoisin sauce
mandarin pancakes or flour tortillas

Marinate the pork with the rice wine vinegar, soy sauce and cornflour. Let stand for 30 minutes.

Cover the mushrooms with hot water and soak for 30 minutes. Clean, rinse, drain and finely shred. Soak the golden needles in hot water for 30 minutes, drain, cut off and discard the hard ends, and cut in thirds. Tie in knots.

Heat 2 tablespoons of the oil in a wok or skillet at medium heat and add the ginger. Scramble the eggs, remove, and cut into fine pieces. Increase the heat, add the remaining tablespoon of oil, and stir-fry the pork. Add the spring onions, wood ears and golden needles; heat through for about 3 minutes. Return the scrambled eggs to the skillet and mix. Spread hoisin sauce on a mandarin pancake or tortilla, add the meat mixture, roll up and eat.
Serves 4

Moroccan-inspired Chicken Tagine

This recipe contains the spice mixture ras-al-hanout, which may include over thirty ingredients, including rosebuds and lavender. Including it gives the dish an authentic Moroccan taste. Including the saffron and orange blossom water, this recipe has four edible flowers as ingredients.

2 chicken breasts, cut into bite-size pieces
1 tbsp flour, season with pinch of salt, pepper and paprika
1 onion, chopped
1 bay leaf
2 cloves garlic, chopped finely

1 tbsp fresh ginger, grated

1 pinch saffron, soaked in a little boiling water for 10 minutes

½ tsp paprika

2 tsp ras-al-hanout spice mix

¼ tsp ground cinnamon

1 cup (240 ml) chicken stock

1 tsp honey

1/3 cup (50 g) dried apricots, halved and soaked in water (Note: to be authentic use apricots but in a pinch you could use dates, or as a last choice raisins)

handful of fresh coriander leaves (cilantro), roughly chopped for garnish

½ tsp orange flower water

Coat the chicken in the flour, heat 2 tbsp oil in a heavy-bottomed casserole dish and brown gently. Remove the chicken and then sauté the onion until it is soft. Add the garlic, ginger, bay leaf and ras-el-hanout spice mix and sauté for another minute. Add the chicken, saffron and stock. Bring to the boil, cover and put in the oven for about 30 to 40 minutes, or until the chicken is cooked. Halfway through the cooking, add the apricots.

When the chicken is cooked, add the honey and orange flower water and cook for a few more minutes. Boil down the juices if too thin, spoon off any excess fat and then add the fresh coriander.

Serve over couscous or rice.

Serves 4

Select Bibliography

Albala, Ken, ed., *The Food History Reader: Primary Sources* (New York, 2014)

Bacher, Miche, *Cooking with Flowers* (Philadelphia, PA, 2013)

Barash, Cathy Wilkinson, *Edible Flowers: From Garden to Palate* (Golden, CO, 1993)

Belsinger, Susan, *Flowers in the Kitchen: A Bouquet of Tasty Recipes* (Loveland, CO, 1991)

Bissell, Frances, *The Scented Kitchen: Cooking with Flowers* (London, 2007)

Brown, Kathy, *The Edible Flower Garden: From Garden to Kitchen* (Wigston, 2011)

Burger, William C., *Flowers: How They Changed the World* (New York, 2006)

Creasy, Rosalind, *The Edible Flower Garden* (Singapore, 1999)

Crowhurst, Adrienne, *The Flower Cookbook* (New York, 1973)

Davidson, Alan, *The Oxford Companion to Food* (New York, 1999)

Freedman, Pail, ed., *Food: The History of Taste* (Berkeley, CA, 2007)

Gibbons, Euell, *Stalking The Healthful Herbs* (New York, 1966)

Laudan, Rachel, *Cuisine & Empire: Cooking in World History* (Berkeley, CA, 2013)

Leggatt, Jenny, *Cooking with Flowers* (New York, 1987)

Leyel, C. F., *Herbal Delights: Tisanes, Syrups, Confections, Electuaries, Robs, Juleps, Vinegards and Conserves* (London, 1937)

Mackin, Jeanne, *Cornell Book of Herbs & Edible Flowers* (Ithaca, NY, 1993)

MacNicol, Mary, *Flower Cookery* (New York, 1967)

McVicar, Jekka, *Cooking with Flowers* (London, 2003)

Morse, Kitty, *Edible Flowers: A Kitchen Companion* (New York, 1995)

Sitwell, William, *A History of Food in 100 Recipes* (New York, 2013)

Smith, Leona Woodring, *The Forgotten Art of Flower Cookery* (Gretna, 1973)

Stewart, Amy, *The Drunken Botanist* (Chapel Hill, NC, 2013)

Tenenbaum, Frances, ed., *Taylor's 50 Best Herbs and Edible Flowers: Easy Plants for More Beautiful Gardens* (New York, 1999)

Websites and Associations

As we were researching this book and discussing it with friends, a frequent comment was, 'I don't have a garden, so I can't make anything with edible flowers.' What we found, however, is that there are lots of options beyond having a garden that allow you to enjoy edible flowers, including foraging, organic produce and farmer's markets. There are also lots of ethnic markets and online resources where products such as flower jams can be purchased. And, if you don't want to be the cook, just keep your eyes open for restaurants that not only garnish with flowers but incorporate them into their dishes, cocktails and desserts. Travel to flower festivals and enjoy flower foods as part of your travel experience.

Gardening resources (including lists of edible flowers, sources of seeds and more)

Two blogs that have wonderful searchable databases by flower with advice as to foraging, precautions and culinary uses of the flowers listed:

http://whatscookingamerica.net/EdibleFlowers/
    EdibleFlowersMain.htm
www.eattheweeds.com

Government and university websites offer lists of edible flowers for specific areas. For example, Colorado State University: www.ext.colostate.edu

Online seed catalogues such as from Thompson and Morgan provide useful lists of edible flowers: www.thompson-morgan.com/edible-flowers

Foraging

Hundreds of organizations are involved in foraging – for example Wild Foodies in Philadelphia: www.meetup.com/Wild-Foodies-of-Philly. Search the web under 'foraging' to find those in your area.

Top ten foraging classes in the UK: www.countryfile.com/countryside/top-10-foraging-courses

On the Internet since 1997, www.foraging.com is a useful, all-inclusive website.

Fresh edible flowers

If you cannot grow it or forage for it, you can probably buy it. Check out organic sections of your local grocery (Whole Foods Market sometimes has seasonal edible flowers available) or farmers' market. You can also buy edible flowers online. Some sites are restricted to restaurant purchases only but others are open to home cooks. Often fresh organic (untreated) flowers cannot be shipped internationally, so check within your country for resources. For example, Greens of Devon sells edible flowers within the UK: www.greensofdevon.com

Westlands in the UK prides itself on having a distinctive collection of edible leaves and flowers, some of which are foraged: www.westlandswow.co.uk

Maddocks Farm Organics, also in the UK, promises overnight delivery of fresh edible flowers suitable for wedding cakes, cocktails, savoury dishes and for crystallization: http://maddocksfarmorganics.co.uk

Edible flower buyers in the U.S. can turn to companies like Gourmet Sweet Botanicals: www.gourmetsweetbotanicals.com; or Chefs Garden:
www.chefs-garden.com

Flower associations

The association that specializes in daylilies is called The American Hemerocallis Society: www.daylilies.org/AHSinfo.html. There are associations for almost any flower offering an abundance of information on growing and using a particular flower of interest. There is even a Clove Spice Association (ACSA) which promotes innovative uses of cloves.

Flower festivals

An Internet search for 'lavender festivals' will turn up dozens of such festivals all around the world. Similar results will be found for other flowers. For example, there is the Bulgarian rose festival that has been going on annually since 1903: http://bulgariatravel. org. There is even a festival for capers in Salina, Italy: www.ataste oftravelblog.com/salinas-caper-festival. Or, for information about festivals and tours of the lavender fields in the south of France, see www.moveyouralps.com, among other such tour websites. Some readers might want to plan a trip around edible flowers. Viet Vision Travel planned the seven-coloured rice trip in Vietnam described in this book:
www.vietvisiontravel.com

Flower products

Even your local grocery store will have many flower products, such as capers or artichokes, but you will often have a bigger selection in ethnic markets. Mediterranean shops will have rose and orange-blossom waters, Chinese markets will have 'golden needles', and Hispanic markets will have hibiscus syrup, to name just a few.

Online there are plenty of sites that specialize in particular edible flower products. For example, dandelion jelly can be purchased from Berkshire Berries, https://shop.berkshireberries.com; dried elderflowers and syrups can be bought at Norm's Farms, http://normsfarms.com; candied flowers can be purchased online at http://shop.gourmetsweetbotanicals.com, and can be used decorate cakes, cookies and other baked goods. Most people find it much easier to buy candied flowers than to tediously make them at home. Crystallized flower petals can rim your next margarita or be used in your futuristic molecular gastronomy creation: http://store.molecularrecipes.com. Confiserie Florian in France produces beautiful floral candies in shops throughout the country and online at www.confiserieflorian.co.uk. Kastulyans, https://kastulyans.com, a landmark shop in New York City for fine speciality foods, sells many dried flower products for teas and every imaginable spice mix.

Acknowledgements

Many people, from all around the world helped us in various ways to put this book together. We would like to acknowledge in particular the assistance of the commissioning editor for the Reaktion Edible series, Andrew Smith; Tom Kirker, our 'enabler' who might never have eaten a flower but for this book; and Joanne Bening, a Philadelphia-based photographer who generously shared her expertise with us.

Several growers and distributors of edible flowers generously gave us their time and invaluable information. Among these were Marjorie Ruggles, the owner and manager of Springthyme Herb Farm in Hockessin, Delaware; Bob Allen and his wife Hue, owners of Golden Garden Produce, Dalat, Vietnam; Farmer Lee Jones, Chef's Garden, Huron Ohio and his staff – Allen, Madison, Michelle, Judy and Ulfetr; Ann Lenhardt from Norm's Farms, Pittsboro, North Carolina; Dona Abramson at Kastulyan's in New York City; and Justin Hulshizer, a saffron grower from Wernersville in Pennsylvania.

We are indebted to the chef Oscar Carrizosa at Casa Crespo in Oaxaca, Mexico; Berndt Brandstatter, the chef at Herwig's Austrian Bistro in State College, Pennsylvania; and the chefs at Chi Hoa restaurant in Ho Chi Minh City, Vietnam; the Boutique Spa Hotel in Sapa, Vietnam; the Yunnan Kitchen in New York City; and the Persian Grill in Lafayette Hill, Pennsylvania.

Katherine Lorenz, PhD, an early reader of the book, gave us both editing and proofreading assistance as did the Friends and Books book club in Cincinnati. Thanks to Charlotte Chu,

Singapore, for her help in researching the pea-flower; to Lynn Oliver from the International Association of Culinary Professionals, editor of The Food Timeline; to the Old Eagle Garden Club, Wayne, Pennsylvania for their support and encouragement; and to the wonderful staff at the St Bernard Branch of the Cincinnati and Hamilton County Public Library who pulled over 400 volumes for us as we conducted our research. Dave Dettman from the University of Pennsylvania and writer of the food blog https://asianmarketsphilly.wordpress.com shared his knowledge of Asian markets with us and the Wild Foodies 'meetup' group in Philadelphia taught us about the joys of foraging for edible flowers.

We would like to thank the staff at Heartwood Acres Mansion, Pittsburgh, Pennsylvania for a wonderful flower luncheon and garden tour and the Institute of Culinary Education in New York City, from whose instructors we learned new uses for floral ingredients. Our thanks also to Tracey at Viet Vision Travel in Hanoi, Vietnam for arranging our seven-coloured rice tour in Sapa.

Finally, we are grateful for the tireless efforts of our editor and book wrangler John Kachuba.

Photo Acknowledgements

The author and publishers wish to express their thanks to the below sources of illustrative material and/or permission to reproduce it.

Bo Basil: p. 81; © The British Library Board: p. 23; Walter Francis Elling: p. 62; Hozinja: p. 103; iStock: p. 6 (Jowita Stachowiak); Constance L. Kirker: pp. 10, 18, 58, 75; Constance L. Kirker/Mary Newman: pp. 8, 9, 12, 22, 32, 41, 42, 56, 59, 63, 65, 66, 67, 74, 76, 84, 86, 92, 97, 98, 102, 106, 109, 114, 116, 117, 120, 126, 128; Ladurée: p. 93; Ann Lenhardt from Norm's Farms: p. 107; poster image by SyracuseCulturalWorkers.com scw © 2009: p. 48; © 2016 United States General Services Administration and California State Parks, Monterey State Historic Park Collection: p. 77; Victoria & Albert Museum, London: p. 123; Yale University Library: p. 46.

Index

italic numbers refer to illustrations; **bold** to recipes

14th of July Salad **141**

Acton, Mrs, *Modern Cookery* 40
Albala, Ken, *Eating Right in the
    Renaissance* 31
Allen, Bob 50, 129
Alma-Tadema, Lawrence,
    The Roses of Heliogabalus
    19
Americas 23, 24, 111–17, 125
    Central America 115
    North America 99, 113,
    118, 119, 122
    South America 24, 115,
    119, 123
Another Sauce for Fowl **139**
aphrodisiacs (love potions) 81,
    87, 105
Apicius, Marcus Gavius 17, 18
Arab 21, 28, 82
artichoke 17, 71, 75–9, *76*
Asia 20–28, 35, 39, 54–88, 108,
    118
Austria 98
ayurveda 21

azalea 132
Aztecs 10, *10*, 23, 24, 111, *112*,
    115, 118

Bach, Edward 43
Baghdad Cookbook 33, 83
banana blossom 65–8, *66, 67*
banana passion fruit 125, *126*
Barash, Cathy Wilkinson,
    *Edible Flowers: From Garden
    to Palate* 118
Bartram, John 113
bee balm 34
Beef with Rosebuds **141–2**
beer 12, 27, 28, 116, 121
Beeton, Mrs Isabella,
    Household Management 40
bell flower (campanula) 87
Bible 14–15, 81–2, 87
bird's tongue *126*, 127
Bissell, Frances, *The Scented
    Kitchen: Cooking with
    Flowers* 40
Black Death *see* plague
Blamanger **140**

Blockwich, Martin, *The Anatomie of the Elder* 105
blue pea flower 69
borage 34, 86, 118
British 33, 39, 41, 52, 65, 94, 99, 110, 122
broccoli 44
Brother Cadfael's Herb Garden 26
Buddha *63, 59,* 65
bugloss 86

cacao (chocolate) 24, 111, 112
calendula 19, 26, 45, 118
Canadian honewort 125, *126*
candying 40, *41,* 89
capers 19, 45, 79–82, *80, 83*
carnation 20, 90
Carson, Rachel, *Silent Spring* 47
cauliflower 44
century plant 24
chamomile 26, 108, *109*
Chardin, Jean-Baptiste, *La Brioche 85*
cherry blossom 70
Child, Julia, *Mastering the Art of French Cooking* 47
China 13, 20–22, 54–65, *56,* 70, 82, 87, 90, 121
chives *109,* 124
chrysanthemum 20, 34, 51, 55–8, *58*
Cixi, Empress Dowager 41, *56,* 61
Clove Island 21
clover *109*

cloves 20, 28, *30,* 33, 40, 45, 54, 121
confit 12, 87, *97*
conquistadores 24, 122, 123
conserve 34, 35, 94, 101, 139
Constantinople 26
cork flower (katary flower) 46
cowslip 93, 108, *109*
crocus 15, 16, 17
Crusades 73, 91
Culpeper, Nicholas, *Complete Herbal* 35, *36*

daisy 34
dandelion 14, 43, 87, *97*
Day of the Dead 117, *117*
daylily (golden needles) 20, 34, 58–60, *59*
Dewitt, David, *Da Vinci's Kitchen* 91
diem diem flower 46
distilling 32, *32,* 83
doctrine of signatures 29
Double Ninth Festival 57, *58*
Dutch 35, 45, 118, 122
dye 119

Ebers Papyrus 16
Egypt, Egyptians 16, 17, 20, 88, 90, 99, 108
El Bulli 51
elderflower 34, 90, 104–8, *106, 107,* 133
Elizabeth I, queen of England 100, *100,* 101
England 73, 99
Ephron, Nora 79

Esquivel, Laura, *Like Water for Chocolate* 90
Europe 89–110, 95, 104, 105, 122, 131
Evelyn, John 106

Fairy Butter **140**
Fantin-Latour, Henri, *Nasturtiums 123*
fennel 19, 34
flor de Izote 125, *126*
flower hotpot *9*
forager 10, *10*, 47, 51, 52
Four Thieves Vinegar 102
France 84, 85, 93, *93*, 94–95, 102, *114,* 129
Fraser, Evan D. G., and Andrew Rimas, *Empires of Food* 27

garden
    Edible Schoolyard 49
    Egyptian *16*
    medieval 27, *27*
    monastery 99
    organic 49–50, 134
    Thomas Jefferson's 78, 124
    victory 44, 47
    Whitehouse *48*, 49
Gardner, Isabella Stewart 125
garnish 9, *12*, 12, 20, 48, 51, 61, 70, *85*, 96, 108, 120, 125, 134
geraniums *109*
Gerard, John, *Herball* 35, *36*

Gibbons, Euell 47, 131, 133
    Stalking the Healthful Herbs 95
Glasse, *Hannah Art of Cookery* 37
goldenrod *126*, 127
Greece, Greeks 16–17, 20, 77, 81, 84, 87, 91, 93, 97, 99

Havasupai Indian Squash Blossom Pudding **142**
herb 11, 14–15, 21, 24, 26, 29, 34–5, 42–4, 50, 52–3, 68, 87, 95, 98–100, 115–16, 122–3, 131, 133, 155
herbes de Provence 102, *102*, 103
Hermes, Pierre *93*, 95
hibiscus (*flor de Jamaica*) 24, 88, 90, 119–21, *120*
    Hibiscus Chutney **145**
Hindu 21, 54–55, 61, *63*
hoa 7
Homer 17
honey 17, 39, 73, 77, 84–86, *86*, 94, 96, 107
hops 27
hyssop (anise) 87

IKEA 108
Inca 24, 123
India 20, 21, 99, 65, 67, 68, 72, 82, 121
Indonesia 69
Industrial Revolution 42
Iran 73
Ireland 109

Israel 85, *81*
Italy 78, 82, 85, 86, 87

jam 50, 94, *97,* 134, 151
Japan 57, 60, 64
jasmine 21, 29
jellies 87, 94, *97,* 108, 109, 110
Jerusalem 79, *81*
Jones, Lee 52, 129
Jove's flower (carnation) 20

kitchen gods 7, *8*
Korea 60, 132

language of flowers
    (floriography) 40, 89–90, 95
lavender 33, 90, 99–104, *103,* 108
lilac 108, *109*
liqueur 12, 50, 94, 98, 105
loroco 126, *126*
lotus 7, 16, 20, 40–41, 61–4,
    62, 65
Lyle, Mrs C. F., *The Gentle Art
    of Cookery* 44

magnolia 112, *126,* 127
mahua flower 69
Malaysia 69
marigolds 35, 53, 115–18, *116,*
    117, *117*
marinade 108
Marshall, Mrs, *Book of Cookery*
    40
Maya 24
medicinal 24–9, 34–5, 77,
    81, 90, 105, 108, 114–15,
    131–4

medicine 14, 21, 27, 99, 111
medieval garden 27
Mediterranean 16, 20, 71–88
Mexico 111–17, 119, 127, 129
Middle Ages 26, 27, 28, 91,
    100
Middle East 21, 26, 28, 71–88,
    90
Minoan 17, 18, *18*
mint 87
molecular gastronomy 8, 12,
    53, 82
monastery 26, 29, 77, 101
Mongol 39
monks 27, 28, 29
Moo Shu Pork 59, *59,* **145–6**
mooncake festival 64
Morocco 82, 84
    Moroccan-inspired
        Chicken Tagine **146–7**
Mughal *38,* 39, 65
Murrell, John, *Two Books
    of Cookeries and Carving*
    93
mustard flower 87

nasturtiums 34, 45, 122–5
neem flower 69
nouvelle cuisine 48

Oaxaca 119
Odyssey 17
okra 88
orange blossom 29, 40, 45,
    82–6, *84, 86*
orchid 132
organic 47, 49–50, 151–2

Pakistan 95
Partridge, John, *The Treasure of Hidden Secrets and Commodious Conceits* 106
pastilles 96
Pennsylvania Dutch 74, 96
peony 34, 70
Persia 16, 20, 39, 74, *74*, 90–91
Peru 24, 115, 122
Philippines 67
Phoenicians 20, 72
pickle 12, 70, 79, 93, 119, 124, 127
Pinkham, Lydia *42, 43*
plague 26, 102
Pliny 77, 98, 105
poinsetta 134
pollen 50, 132
poppy 37
pot marigold 19, 26, 34, 118
primrose 26, 34, 108
Provence 103

Queen Anne's Lace 133
Queen's Closet Opened 101
quilitl 23

Ramayana *23*
Recipes for 22 Ailments 21
redbud 127
Roman 17–19, 72, 77, 84–5, 91, 93, 99, 105, 131
rose 19–21, 34, 50, 51, 90–95, *92*, 118, **139–40**
rosebuds 33, **141–2**
    Rose Petal Sorbet **143–4**

rose sugar 96
rosewater 32–4, 40, 45, 54, 83, 91–2, 94, **140**

saffron 15–17, 19, 29–33, *31*, 40, 54, 68, 71–75, *74*
Saffron Walden 73, *75*
sage flower 34
    Sage-flower Mustard **144**
Sanskrit 22
Sapa 22
scape 108, 109, *109*
seven-coloured rice 22
Shennong 20, 21, 133
Shore, Harriet *Artichoke Pickers 77*
Silk Road 20, 72
Singapore 69, *116*
Sita 22, 23, *23*
Smith, Leona Woodring, *Forgotten Art of Flower Cookery* 123
snapdragon 132
Song of Solomon 15, 72
sorrel 108, *109*
South Africa 24
Spain 73, 77, 83, 84, 85, 108
spice blends 12, 28, 87, 102
spikenard 99
Spry, Constance, *Come into the Garden Cook* 46
squash 113–14, *114*, 118
St Germain 105, *106*
Stein, Gertrude 45, *46*
sugar 34, 39, 50, 61, 64, 92–6, 98, 102, 104, 108, 118–21
Sumerian 15, 72, 81

symbol 21, 57, *63*, 64, 68–9, 84, *85*, 89–92, 95, 99, 109, 116, 118
syrup 12, 33, *38*, 39, 50, 54, 69, 96, 104–5, *106*, 107–8, 154

Tang Dynasty *37*, 38, 70
tea 42, 55–6, 61, 70, 94, 96, 99, *99*, 108–10
    artichoke 78
    chamomile 108
    elderflower 104, 107
    five-flower *56*
    herbal 61, 78
    hibiscus 119, 121, 132
    lavender 101
    Liberty 127
    marigold 115, 118
Tet 7, *8*
Thailand 67
three sisters 113
Toklas, Alice B. 45, *46*, **141**
torch ginger flower 69
toxic 21, 131–4
traditional medicine 21
Tu Duc, Emperor 41–2
tulip 45
Turkey 77, 79, 82, 129
Turkish pastries *84*

United States 43, 49–50, 78, 85–6, 94, 107, 114, 120–23, 127, 132

Victoria, queen of the UK 85, 96, 104
Victorian era 40–44, *41*, 89, 94

victory garden 44, 47
Vietnam 7, 8, 21, *22*, 40, 46, 50, *66*, 69–70, *76*, 129
vinegar 93, 94, 102, 106, 108, 110
violet 34, 90, 93, 95–9, *98*
    Violet Pineapple Soup **143**

wasabi flowers *128*, 129
Wasson, R. G., *The Wondrous Mushroom* 111
Waters, Alice 48–9
Whiteman, Robin, *Brother Cadfael's Herb Garden* 26
Whole Foods Market 50
wine 12, 15, 19, 21, 55–7, *58*, 87, 90–91, 93, 97–8, 108–9

yucca plant 24

Ziedrich, Linda, *The Joy of Jams, Jellies and other Sweet Preserves* 94